KT-570-622

Elmina's Kitchen

Elmina's Kitchen received its British premiere at the Royal National Theatre, London on 29 May 2003. The cast was as follows:

Digger	Shaun Parkes
Deli	Paterson Joseph
Anastasia	Dona Croll
Ashley (*Deli's son*)	Emmanuel Idowu
Baygee	Oscar James
Clifton	George Harris

Director Angus Jackson
Designer Bunny Christie
Lighting Designer Hartley TA Kemp
Music Neil McArthur
Sound Designer Neil Alexander
Company Voice Work Patsy Rodenburg
Dialect Coach Claudette Williams
Musicians Steve Russell, Juldeh Camaram, Atongo Zimba
Original Songs Kwame Kwei-Armah, Neil McArthur, George Harris, Oscar James

Prologue

The stage is in darkness. A single spotlight slowly reveals a costumed man, standing absolutely still with a gurkel (a one-string African guitar famed for possessing the power to draw out spirits) in his hands. His head moves sharply as if smelling something distasteful. The music starts. It is a slow lament-sounding concoction of American blues and traditional African music.

The man then covers the length and breadth of the stage flicking handful amounts of powder on to the playing area. The music ends.

Blackout.

Scene One

It's Tuesday, mid-afternoon. It's raining. We are in Elmina's Kitchen, a one-notch-above-tacky West Indian food takeaway restaurant in 'Murder Mile' Hackney. The walls are littered with 'Dance Hall' advertisements and Whey and Nephew-type posters. Amid the Budweiser series of posters celebrating African-American heroes there is a big sign saying 'NO DRUGS ARE PERMITTED ON THESE PREMISES. RESPECT.' The TV that is attached to the left wall closest to the counter is blaring out the ragga tune 'Sufferer' by Bounty Killer. To the right is a rack of spirits. There is a telephone on the counter. Behind the counter are two wooden swing doors that lead to the kitchen. Above that is a huge picture of an middle-aged West Indian woman, Elmina, **Deli***'s mother. Next to that is a framed laminated poster that reads, 'Life is beauty, admire it. Life is costly, care for it. Life is wealth, keep it. Life is love, enjoy it. Life is a dream, realise it. Life is a challenge, meet it. Life is a duty, serve it. Life is a game, play it. Life is a mystery, know it. Life is an opportunity, benefit from it. Life is a promise, fulfil it.'*

Standing behind the counter is **Deli** *(thirty-four), a happy spirit. He is a born struggler and self-optimist, but today he is a little restless. Although slightly overweight, we can see that he once possessed a fit, athletic body. Personality-wise he is soft at the core. He has his head* *buried deep in a letter while mouthing the words to the song being played on the TV. 'Born as a sufferer, grow up as a sufferer, struggle as a sufferer, fe mek it as a sufferer, fight as a sufferer, survive as a sufferer, move amongst the ghetto ah most ah dem ah sufferer ah!', etc., etc.*

When he raises his head we see that he has a big bruise above his eye and a few cuts on his forehead.

Sitting on a stool close to the counter is **Digger** *(mid-thirties). He is very powerfully built and looks every bit the 'bad man' that he is. His hair is plaited in two neat sets of cane rows which meet each other at the top of his head. At the ends of the cane rows are multicoloured ribbons, the kind traditionally seen in young girls' hair.* **Digger** *is from Grenada but came to England aged fourteen. His clothes are not flash but are name-brand street clothes. The Chopper bicycle that we see chained outside the restaurant is his.* **Digger***'s accent swings from his native Grenadian to hard-core Jamaican to authentic black London. He has his hands-free adapter permanently plugged into his ear. He is busy reading the* Daily Mirror.

Digger *(to himself but loud)*   You mudder arse!

Deli *glances up at* **Digger** *and then to the picture of his mother.*

Deli *(as if on autopilot)*   How many times I got to tell you about language like that in here, Digger?

He returns to the letter. **Digger** *raises his head from his paper momentarily and gently kisses his teeth in* **Deli***'s direction. He's got to get back to the article.* **Deli** *finishes reading the letter, screws it up and throws it in the bin. Suddenly* **Digger** *shouts out.*

Digger *(in disbelief)*   Blood CLATT.

Deli *(irritated)*   Digger!

Digger   What?

Deli   Ah you me ah talk too yuh na!

Digger *(vexed)*   You can't see dat I reading som'ting?

He ignores **Deli** *and carries on reading.*

Deli   Man, you're ignorant!

Digger *doesn't like being called ignorant.*

Digger (*half playful*)   Char! You only lucky I don't want eat wid dem drug-selling niggas down Yum Yums, why I don't boo you down and tek my business dere. Gimme fritter an a Ginness punch.

Deli   Please!

Digger   What's wrong wid you today?

Deli   Cos I ask you to say please something must be wrong with me? See my point? You're ignorant.

He brings the fritter and the punch he has poured out over to **Digger**.

Two pound twenty-five. Please.

Digger (*checking his pockets*)   Give me a squeeze na?

Deli (*almost laughing*)   Squeeze? You *own* more money than anyone I know.

Digger   But dat's my business, Deli.

Deli   Just gimme me fucking money.

Digger   See you. You coming jus' like your cousin Sofie, a rhated Englishman.

Deli *pauses for a moment, confused.*

Deli   Please explain to me how my female cousin, can be a white male?

Digger   You know what I mean, she love too much blasted Englishman. (*Shaking his head.*) You British blacks, boy.

He shows him a picture of her in the paper.

Every time she dey in the paper, she have a rhated white man on she hand. Wha' appen! Ghetto willy too big fe her or what?

Deli What the hell that has to do with putting your mean hand in your pocket to pay for your fritters? It's low-life dregs like you that probably send her dere.

Digger (*taking umbrage*) Low what? See me and you, we go fall out one day, you know! I not no low nothin'. I's a legitimate businessman!

Deli You forget I know where the butcher knife is!

Digger *pulls out his gun and points it at* **Deli**.

Digger Yeah, but what's that gonna do against my tech. nine, motherfucker?

Deli (*vexed*) Don't fuck about, Digger, how you gonna be pulling that ting out in here? . . .

Digger . . . Sorry! Sorry! . . .

The phone rings.

Deli . . . What happen if a customer walk in now? I done told you about that x amount a times. Damn. Hello! Elmina's Kitchen, takeaway and delivery, how can I help you? . . . Chicken? We have jerk chicken, curried chicken, fried chicken, brown chicken, stew chicken and our new vibe is sweet and sour chicken. Yeah, West Indian style . . . Yeah, yeah . . . Where'd you live, bra? Berringham Road, seen, gonna be forty-five minutes, you alright wid dat? . . . What's your name? Badder youth? Seen, Badder, that'll be five pounds fifty cash handed over to my delivery boy before he takes the food out of the heated rear box, yeah? Nice.

Digger *who has returned to the paper, looks up at* **Deli** *and shakes his head.*

Digger Da'is why you nigger people go fail every time. How you go tell a hungry man he have to wait forty-five minutes for he food?

Deli (*shouting from the kitchen*) You can't run a business on lies.

Digger   You think a Indian man would do that? That's why the black man will always be down. He don't know how to analyse his environment.

Deli   What graffiti wall did you get that from, Digger?

Digger   Your mudder's. Sorry!

He bites into his fritter. He grimaces.

Bombo! Deli, your cooking is shit! How can a man fuck up a fritter?

Deli (*smiling*)   Don't watch that, Dougie reach and you know his cooking is baddd!

Digger   What! He's gonna sit down in the kitchen and cook? Ha ha!

The phone rings.

Deli   Elmina's Kitchen, takeaway and delivery, how can I help you? . . . Sweet and sour chicken? . . . Where'd you live, bra? . . .

He looks up at **Digger** *and hesitates for a moment.*

Deli   Well, that'll be . . . that'll be the next one out. Yeah, yeah, respect.

Digger *laughs at him.*

Digger   See, I told yu' you was coming like dem English man. Fork-tongued motherfucker.

Deli (*feigning ignorance*)   What? Man, since I've put that sweet and sour shit on the menu the phone's been off the hook.

Digger   I don't mean to be disrespectful but your shop is never, has never and I doubt will ever be, off the hook.

Deli   Some things shouldn't be measured in financial terms.

Digger   A business is one of those thing that should!

Deli (*kisses his teeth*)   Digger, fuck off.

Digger   Oh, it's alright for you to use all manner of Viking exple, exples, swear word, but as soon as a motherfucker uses language of our heritage you start to cuss. Dat is what I talking about when I cuss you British blacks.

Deli *kisses his teeth and ignores* **Digger**. **Digger**'*s phone rings. He takes out three. He finds the right one. He switches his accent to hard-core Jamaican.*

Digger   Yeah, yeah? Tricky wha you say, rude bwoy? . . . Seen . . . Seen . . . Na!!! Wha you ah say? . . . . Alright . . . usual tings ah go run . . . seen . . . tie him up wait for me . . . Tricky, don't be a pussy and get trigger happy, wait for me, you hear? Alright, what is it, three now? I'll see you 'bout four thirty. Later . . .

He ends the call.

I gotta get myself some new blood. Tricky stewpid!

Deli   Thought you was a lone operator?

Digger   I subcontract on a job-by-job basis. Eh, you know who I had business with de odder day? Spikey!

Deli (*not really interested*)   Spikey who?

Digger   Spikey, who own the hair shop down by Stamford Hill lights.

Deli (*suddenly interested*)   What Roy's from across the road big mouth friend with the hair? You lie?

Digger   Oh ho! You interested now?

Deli   Who Spikey did owe money?

Digger   Me!

Deli   Before you, fool?

Digger   Matic posse.

Deli   I knew that motherfucker had to be dealing. How else could he move from one fucking blow-dryer and Sat'day girl to employing twelve fit woman in under nine months?

Digger   I thought you doesn't watch odder people tings?

Deli   Shut up. How much was he down for?

Digger   Nothin' real big. Twenty.

Deli   Twenty?

Digger   Well, he owe Matic dem fifteen and once I put my fee pon top . . .

Deli   . . . Twenty? Damn.

Digger   When I put de gun by he head, you know what he do?

Deli   What?

Digger   He offer me him fifteen-year-old daughter?

Deli   To do what wid?

Digger   To fuck of course.

Deli (*outraged*)   You lie?

Digger   I buck him with me pistol. Who the hell you take me for, Rodent?

Deli   Rodent?

Digger   The Yardie bwoy that rape all them people dem pickney when he was collecting. Motherfucker gave the trade a bad name.

Deli   Ras! He pay yuh you money yet?

Digger   I told him I'd kill his family across the whole world. He had my money to me in five days.

Deli   So that's why the shop's closed!

Digger I give him an extra lick cos me did hear he was an informer.

Deli Yeah? Fucking bitch. Should'a give him two.

The men sing together.

Deli/Digger Man fe dead lick a shot inna informer man hend.

Enter **Ashley**, *his son (nineteen), hooded street clothes, headphones. He has his hair in two bunches. Trousers falling off the arse. Has no respect for anyone older than himself except for* **Digger**. *He walks in slowly talking on the phone.*

Deli Yo! Ashley, what took you so long? How you let the man cut up your head so? Look like Zorro.

The men laugh together. **Ashley** *kisses his teeth, grabs the TV remote off the counter, changes the channel to MTV base and attempts to sit down.*

Deli What you sitting down for? Can't you see there's ting waiting here to get delivered?

Ashley *looks at his dad's cut head.*

Ashley *(nonchalantly)* It's raining out there, you know! Give me a second to catch my breath.

Deli You wanna catch you arse out street and deliver the people dem food.

Ashley Nigger needs to chill, boy!

Deli Hey, I ain't no nigger with you.

Ashley *(to himself almost)* No you're not, what they calling you on street now? Deli the sissy punk.

Deli What?

Ashley How am I supposed to walk the street an look my bredrens in the eye when mans all grip up my dad by his throat and you didn't deal wid it?

Digger (*still confused*)   What?

Deli *doesn't answer.* **Ashley** *does.*

Ashley   Roy from over dere coarse up my dad . . .

Deli   . . . Coarse up who? . . .

Ashley   . . . and he didn't even lift a finger to defence. Can you believe that?

Digger   You let Roy da coolie coarse you up?

Ashley   . . . (*under breath but loud enough to be heard*) It's a good thing uncle Dougie's coming home that's my word . . .

Deli   . . . He never coarse me nothin'. We had a little someting . . .and I decided not to deal wid it THERE and THEN.

The guys stare at him in amazement.

Digger   Rasclaat!

Deli (*to* **Ashley**)   Me will deal wid him right! What?! I can't see me fucking brodder! Is pass me must pass him in the jail van? (*Beat.*) Did you buy the banner ting for your uncle?

Deli*'s explanation has meant nothing to him.* **Ashley** *slams a big roll of banner tape on counter and pushes it towards his father.*

Deli   Thank you.

Ashley *looks at the address he has to deliver to.*

Ashley   Berrington Road? I ain't delivering no cold food there. Trust me. You better heat it up dread or no can do!

Deli (*sharp and fast*)   Who you talking to like that? Don't mek me have to lick you down you know! Your mouth too quick these days.

Ashley *pushes out his chest.* **Deli** *catches himself, pulls back and takes the container back into the kitchen, kissing his teeth.* **Ashley**

nods his head to **Digger** *who just about acknowledges him.* **Ashley** *pauses for a moment then approaches* **Digger**.

Ashley   So, yes my don, what a gwan?

Digger (*back to reading his paper*)   Just cool ya.

Ashley   You still busting the TT?

Digger (*short*)   Yep.

Ashley   Sweet but when I get my dollars, mine's a BM boy. You done know!

Digger *does not reply.*

Ashley (*checking to see that his dad can't hear*)   Listen, I kinda wanna talk some tings through wid you, you na mean?

Digger   No, I don't know what you mean.

Ashley (*taken aback but bounces back*)   Seen, seen. You're hooked up and dat, and mans needs to get hold of proper tings, not no air pistols runnings, you get me? So I wondered if . . .

Digger (*firmly*)   . . . No.

Ashley   No what?

Digger   No.

Ashley (*with attitude*)   What what? Mans ain't looking a free tings, you know!

Digger   Yes you is. Don't ever be forward enough to ask me about tings like that again, seen?

Ashley   Seen.

Enter **Deli**. *Hands food to* **Ashley**.

Deli   Take it na! And hurry come back. You gotta to help me sort the room for your uncle.

Ashley *does but he's staring at* **Digger** *as he exits.* **Digger** *takes the remote and puts it back on to the old school music channel.*

Digger   Dem blasted young children duh' have no respect. You know, some parts ah de country fucking big man like you and me 'fraid to come out dey yard because young punks like him wanna shot dem down to get stripes? Not me a rass!

Deli *stares at the door that* **Ashley** *just exited with great concern in his eyes.*

Deli   What! . . . .

Enter **Baygee***, a hyper lively old Bajan man in his sixties who often speaks at a hundred miles an hour. He's the last of West Indian door-to-door salesmen. Defying logic he is carrying about twenty different designer bags. He is wearing a three-piece suit with trilby hat to match that have all seen better days. We can see his long grey hair sticking out of the sides. He rushes into the restaurant.*

Baygee   Hey, Delroy, give me a quick shot of Clark's and have one you yourself, I win ten pounds on the lottery today. What James Brown say? (*Sings.*) I feel good, dadadada, I knew that I would now.

Deli   You still playing that stupidness?

Baygee   Be happy for a fella na! You know how many years I giving them people me money and never get fart back?

Deli   Congratulations, Baygee.

Baygee   Thank you. I have some niceeeeeeee new clothes for the children this week, you know, Deli. (*He searches to find the right bag.*) Tracksuits, jeans, baggy trouser that show dey underpants, nice tings, boy. I even have a Donna Karen Los Angeles dress for the wife . . .

Deli   New York.

Baygee   She on holiday?

Deli   Donna Karen New Y . . . Forget it. And it's the ex-wife, Baygee.

Baygee (*smiles*)   Even more reason why you should buy it.
Anyway take a look through, I coming back. Just popping to
see Ms Mary on Abbots Road.

He decks the shot of rum in one.

Deli (*knowing full well*)   She have something for you?

Baygee (*trying to front*)   She owe me twenty pound.

Digger (*teasing him*)   I'll buy that debt off you for fifteen
pound.

Baygee   White boy, I wouldn't sell you my stepmodder
piss, and she been dead twenty years, God bless her soul.
Give me one more, Deli.

*He selects the bags he's going to walk with and makes for the door. He
looks at the picture of Elmina and turns back to* **Deli**.

Oh God, how many times I have to tell you? I love that you
have you modder up there but you need to have one of
yourself too. You could have been one of the greatest, boy.
Clifton took me to see him fight once and I said, Cliff, he
could be one of the greats, you know. He smiled and said, I
know. Put up the picture, boy.

Deli   Soon, Baygee. Soon. Your usual curry goat and rice?

Baygee   Who cook?

Deli   Me!

Baygee   Na, just line me up a patty and a Guinness
punch. In fact, make that two Guinness punch. I go need a
little energy when I leave Ms Mary's. I gone.

He's gone.

Digger   You British blacks, boy.

Deli   And I don't know why you gots to be dissing us all
the time, you been here since you was blasted fourteen,
you're as 'British' as the rest of us.

Digger (*shoots out*)   Never! I was born in Grenada and I've lived in jailhouse all over the world. I know who the fuck I am, don't you ever include me in all you stupidness.

Deli   Five years in a New York jail don't make you a citizen of the world, motherfucker.

Deli *starts to tidy up.* **Digger** *takes the remote control for the TV and points it towards the screen attempting to change the channel. It doesn't work.*

Digger   How you get this thing on the news again?

Deli   You got to watch the news every time it's on? Square then tick.

Digger   What happens up there today, happens on the streets tomorrow.

The news channel is on. **Digger** *is really concentrating.*

We hear the chime that accompanies the opening of the shop's door. The boys look up. Enter **Anastasia** *(forty-two). Although dressed soberly, we can see that she has the kind of body that most men of colour fantasise about. Big hips and butt, slim waist and full, full breasts. There is something incredibly sexual about her presence. Beneath the very well applied 'make-up' we can see that she must once have been a real beauty. There is an insecurity, a soft sadness about her even though she attempts to hide this with a veneer of coarse West Indian confidence. Although black British, she too swings into authentic, full-attitude Jamaican at the drop of a hat. She speaks with confidence if not a little attitude.*

Anastasia *scans the shop quickly then pauses for a second. Then, as if she is somehow rooted to the spot, looks around again but this time slower, more deliberate, as if trying to see something that is not visible, something that is hiding. Subtly, she inhales slowly and then exhales. She snaps out of it and genuinely smiles at* **Deli**. *She has a bag in her hands.*

Anastasia (*firm and confident*)   Hi! I come to apply for the job in the window.

Deli/Digger   Really!

Anastasia   No, I just like opening me mouth and talking stupidness!

The boys clock each other.

Deli   Right, um, you have any experience?

Anastasia, *full of natural sexiness, walks and puts her bag on the counter. She takes out a Pyrex dish of macaroni pie and steps back.*

Anastasia   Macaroni pie. I cooked it yesterday, but next morning food is always the sweetest.

Digger (*half under his breath*)   Mind she obea you, boy!

Deli   Shut up, Digger!

Deli   So you've worked in an West Indian restaurant before?

Anastasia (*almost winking*)   No. But I figure it's not beyond me!

Deli (*a little surprised*)   What makes you would want to work here?

Anastasia   The truth? You're in serious trouble my bredren! Anyone that names his restaurant Elmina's Kitchen is in need of help. The good news! It's the help that I can give . . .

Deli   Elmina's my mother's name!

Digger   Ras!

Deli   And your name is?

Anastasia   Anastasia, it's the name of a princess. Brudder, you can't have a picture of a woman on the wall and the place look so! But what really makes me wanna work here! You is the best-looking man I have seen in a very long time.

Digger *looks up.*

Deli (*taken aback*)   Really?

Anastasia   No, but I knew that would sweet you. So how about you taste my macaroni pie na?

Deli   Are you smoking rock?

Anastasia (*shakes her head*)   No, I don't do drugs and I don't drink.

Deli   . . . Cos, girl, you got brass balls coming in here and tell me about my mudder! People have dead for less.

Digger   True!

Beat.

Anastasia (*seriously*)   Forgive me, I have a warped sense of humour.

Pause.

Deli *takes off the top of the Pyrex dish.* **Anastasia** *takes a pre-package plastic spoon from her bag and hands it to* **Deli**. *She also takes her book out and clenches it like a Bible. It is* The Celestine Prophecy.

Anastasia   Don't you want to heat it up?

Deli *shakes his head. He tastes the pie.* **Digger** *shakes his head.*

Deli   Ummmm, that's good . . . wicked in fact. Wow. You got anything else in there?

Anastasia   I have a goat ready for stewing.

Deli (*gets serious*)   Well, it's a full-time post we have here. It may not look busy now but it can get real rushed at lunchtimes.

Digger *coughs.*

Deli   And we have a reputation in the area for excellence.

Anastasia   So, you offering me the job?

Deli   Why, don't you want it?

Anastasia   You know what I mailed my son last night? I tell him that me walk into a restaurant named after a slave castle but couldn't see the castle.

Deli *doesn't quite know how to respond.*

Digger (*exclaims*)   Rasclaat!

Deli (*ignoring*)   So, when can you start?

Anastasia   Whenever.

Deli   Thursday? . . .

Anastasia (*before it's come out of his mouth*)   . . . Thursday? Fine.

She gathers her things and gets up to leave.

Do you read?

Deli   What do you mean?

Anastasia   How you does feed your mind if you don't read? Typical man.

Deli   I haven't mentioned pay?

Anastasia   It's gonna be more than I'm earning now, right!

He nods. She exits.

Digger (*getting out of his seat*)   That's a rasclatt madwoman! How you could employ dat?

Deli (*ignoring*)   Digger, shut up, man.

Digger (*sitting back down*)   Rhated madwoman.

Lights down.

During the blackout we hear the voice of the **Newsreader**.

Newsreader   The headlines. As the case of John and Peter Goodyear enters it's fifth day at the Old Bailey the brothers go on record saying they murdered their parents 'for the hell of it'. We talk to Denton Philips, the Jamaican gangster, or 'Yardie', brought into Britain by the Metropolitan Police to supposedly help in the fight against crime. And thirty-five million pounds of personal assets were seized from celebrated Ranter frontman, William Forsheve, in the biggest pension scandal to hit the private sector in a decade. (*Music.*) Scenes of astonishment at the Old Bailey today as a spokesman for the two brothers . . .

The lights slowly come up to reveal:

Scene Two

Baygee, Digger *watching the TV. The fourth screw is in. They have glasses of rum in their hand.* **Anastasia** *and* **Deli** *are putting the finishing touches to the 'Welcome Home' decorations for Dougie while watching the TV when they can. The freshly painted banner reads 'Yes, dread, you reach! Respect due!'* **Anastasia** *steps down from a chair and heads towards the kitchen. The restaurant looks a little cleaner. Nothing serious but it looks better.*

Digger   Thirty-five million, you know!

Baygee (*conversationally*)   My father use to say when a black man tief one man cry, when the European dem tief, whole continents bawl. (*Holding up the rum glass to* **Deli**.) Give me one last quick one.

Deli *heads behind the counter to do it.*

Deli   No problem. (*Referring to banners.*) What you think, Baygee?

Baygee   Look good.

Digger   How's a man suppose to enjoy his food when all he can smell is paint to bloodclaat?

Anastasia (*referring to decorations*)   Yes, dread, you reach, now there's a fitting welcome for a black man. 'Bout welcome home.

Deli (*smiling at her*)   OK, you were right.

Anastasia   My God, these tablecloth, Renk! . . . You worse than my son. If I don't change the bedclothes he'll sleep on the same ting for a year!

Digger *and* **Baygee** *clock each other.* **Digger** *puts out his hand.*

Digger   One week before he sex that! Twenty pound.

Deli *hears and looks up at* **Digger** *disapprovingly.* **Baygee** *ignores him.*

Baygee   What time you brodder reaching?

Deli (*kisses his teeth*)   Ahh you know Dougie, he said today *sometime* but I'll believe it when I see him.

He smiles, excited at the prospect.

Baygee   You shouldn't make the boy find he own way home, you should'da pick him up from the gates?

Deli (*flash of anger*)   Alone, is how he wants to come out.

Digger   Yo! Gal, gimme me a next dumpling.

Anastasia (*flash of temper*)   Is who you talking to so? Cos believe, it better not be me.

Digger *is slightly taken aback.* **Deli** *jumps straight in.*

Deli   I bet a hundred pound it's informer business that catch that thirty-five million man.

Digger   Your money would be better spent teaching you staff how to talk to people. (*Changing back to subject at hand.*) Informer, yes!!

Deli   Better you shot me before you ask me fe do that.

Anastasia *stares at* **Deli**, *disappointed. He recoils slightly.*

Digger   Dem man dere, you don't even waste bullet pon dem. (*Imitating stabbing.*) Just jook jook jook him till he dead.

Anastasia   Take it that's why they call you Digger?

Digger   Yep. It tells people who the fuck *I* am and what I do! Ask any nigger in the street and they'll tell you! Digger's like one of them African names. It's got meaning. Remember that!

Anastasia *gets the dumpling from the heated cabinet. She brushes past* **Deli** – *their bodies touch momentarily* – **Deli** *steps back, and looks away.*

Baygee (*annoyed at* **Digger***'s boasting*)   What you do, young white bwoy, is buy and sell black souls!

Digger   I buy and sell debts. Not no cheap-arse fake designer clothes, like some motherfuckers I know.

Baygee   Don't test me, young man. I lash a man last week and he is still falling down!

Deli   Baygee, cool na!

Baygee   Once upon a time, businessmen like me were the only street salesmen our community had. Now look what they got! You may frighten all them others round here, I don't 'fraid you young bad-johns. I hate you, but God blimey, I don't 'fraid you.

Digger (*about to get vexed*)   Wha?!!!

Anastasia *jumps in.*

Anastasia   Digger! Your dumpling! And here (*slams down a glass of rum*), cool your spirits na!

Beat while the men cool down. **Deli** *clocks that* **Anastasia** *saved the moment. He smiles at her.*

The phone rings. **Deli** *picks it up.*

Deli   Hello Elmina's Kitchen, takeaway and delivery, how can I help you? . . . Ashley, what you phoning me on the business line for? Call me on the mobile.

He puts down the phone. **Anastasia** *looks to* **Deli***.* **Deli** *smiles, half apologising for his ignorance. His mobile rings.*

Deli   Yes, who's calling? . . . (*Gets serious.*) Yeah, mate, your uncle's been here an hour already . . . Upstairs . . . (*Vexed.*) Tell him what? . . . I'm not telling him nothing . . . No! I don't know if we'll be here when you finally decide to arrive!

He puts down the phone. **Anastasia** *exhales, shaking her head.*

Deli   Ani, I ain't seen the boy in three days, his uncle is due out and he ain't got the manners to be here first thing in the morning to greet him! Let the bitch stew.

Anastasia *doesn't comment but you can see that she disagrees.*

Anastasia   But he's a bwoy, Deli, dem do tings so.

Deli   Thanks. Think we're all done here? I'm gonna go and get ready.

Anastasia   What's wrong with what you've got on?

Deli   Need to put on something that hides the weight, mate.

Anastasia   You look good to me.

Anastasia *smiles.* **Deli** *stops for the briefest of moments and then carries on. As he steps through the swing doors* **Digger** *picks up the TV remote and switches the TV on to the horseracing channel.* **Anastasia** *(who has just picked up her book) automatically turns to the TV screen.* **Deli**, *however, knew* **Digger** *would do this and pops his head back round the swing doors. He clocks that* **Anastasia** *is paying a lot of attention to the horses.*

Anastasia   Gwan!

She turns away from the TV screen when she hears **Deli**'s *voice.*

Deli (*ignorant*)   Take the horse gambling off, Digger. Ladbroke's is up the bloody road. How many times do I have to tell you?

Digger *turns it back on to MTV base, looks at* **Anastasia** *and indicates to* **Deli**.

Digger   Him luck salt.

Baygee   Turn that ting down, boy.

Digger *takes out a packet of cigarettes and offers one to*
Anastasia. *She picks up her book and reluctantly accepts. She steps*
from behind the counter. He lights it for her.

Digger   Your face is very familiar to me. We meet in a
bashment or something?

Anastasia   Bashment? (*Touch of bitterness.*) All the nice
dance close up or full up wid pickney. I don't rave.

Digger   You don't drink, you don't rave. Wait, wait, I get
it, I get it. I see you wid Bobbler and dem, don't it?

Anastasia   I don't move wid no crack crew!

Digger   Then how you know it's crack dey does run?

Anastasia (*stutters a little*)   Everybody know dat? (*Recovering,*
goes on the front foot.) Wait, what you trying to say? Me look
like one straygay street gal to you?

Digger   You's a feisty thing, innit? That's the way me like
them. Ride better when them have a little spirit. What you
say, Baygee?

Baygee   Why you don't leave the woman alone?

Digger   Wha?! I just getting to know Deli gal.

Anastasia (*aggressively*)   Who tell you that I was Deli's gal?

Digger   No one.

Anastasia   Young bwoy, I doubt if you could ah handle
it. Excuse!

Anastasia *stubs the cigarette out semi-hiding the ashtray and exits*
through the swing door into the kitchen, picking up a pen in the process.

Baygee (*prodding* **Digger**)   Eh, I see a couple of wild Yard
boys driving up a one-way street yesterday. When a man
show them the sign, the youth don't just take out he gun and
threaten to kill him!

Digger *doesn't reply.*

Baygee   Figure it must be one of the new set of Yardies that eating up Hackney. They giving children BMWs, who could compete with that, eh? Hmm! People should always read street signs, don't you think, Digger? I gone. Tell Deli I'll pass back and pay on my way back from Mrs Alexander's house.

He exits with his bags. **Deli** *enters the restaurant dressed in black shirt and pants. He even has a black tie on but not done up. He rolls his head like a boxer preparing for a fight.* **Digger** *looks at him.* **Anastasia** *comes out after* **Deli***, she looks approvingly at him.*

Digger   Bloodclatt, who dead? Where you going dress up so?

Deli   I ain't dress up, just wanna look good for my bra, innit? I spouse up the place, so wah! I can't spouse up meself?

Anastasia   Yes, man, you looks goooooods. Hold up.

She straightens **Deli***'s tie so that it is hanging around his chest.* **Deli** *is not comfortable with her doing this.*

(*Straight, almost motherly.*) Now you look 'ready'.

Digger   Na na, you right, man should meet his brodder the right way and dat and it's nice that you clean up the place for him, but if you'd have come to me, I'd have give you the money to do it up proper, you know big picture of Haile Selassie, next to yuh modder, proper bamboo furniture, dim lighting and such!

Deli   Thanks but if I ever want to do that, I'll go to the bank.

Digger *bursts out laughing.*

Deli   What you laughing at?

Digger   What bank is going to give you money, nigger?

Deli   One that could recognise I've been a businessman from morning . . .

Digger   . . . And one that ignores your black skin?

Deli   Ahhhhh fuck that old school shit Digger. That was some old eighties shit you talking.

Anastasia *goes to the kitchen. Enter* **Ashley**. *His hair has been done. Neat cane rows. He's aware he looks good. He's vexed.*

Deli   So you decide to show up?

Ashley   I can't believe it. See, Dad, I told you you shoulda deal wid that Roy.

Deli   That subject's dead, Ashley.

Ashley   They've not only gone and bought the Chini restaurant shop next to theirs.

Digger *looks away.* **Anastasia** *clocks this.*

Deli   What's the matter wid that?

Ashley (*surprised*)   You ain't read the note, have you?

He produces it out of his back pocket.

'Sorry for the temporary closure, reopening soon as Roy's West Indian restaurant.' They're taking the piss out of you.

Ashley *stares at* **Deli** *with hate in his eyes,* **Digger** *looks away.* **Deli** *rolls his head, clicks his neck. We can see the rage in his eyes. He clocks* **Anastasia** *and tries to cover it.*

Deli   Hey, it's a free world, man, people can do what they want.

Ashley   He takes away your pride, then your livelihood, and all you can do is stand dere like a fish? You've lost it, blood.

Deli (*flash of temper*)   I'm not no blood wid you.

Ashley   Regrettably, that's exactly what you are.

Anastasia *exits to the kitchen.*

Ashley   Char! Where's Uncle D?

Deli   He ain't here yet.

Ashley   I thought you said . . .

Deli (*quickly*)   . . . Don't worry about what I said. You ain't seen your uncle in seven years and the day he's due out you can't be bothered to get your arse here to greet him . . .

Ashley   I had runnings . . .

Deli   . . . Runnings is more important than being here for your uncle?

Ashley *does not reply.*

Deli   So, it's not just me that lets the family down is it?

Beat. **Ashley**'*s face drops.* **Anastasia** *walks into the kitchen.* **Deli** *feels a little guilty so tries to change the subject a bit.*

You see your child today?

Ashley   Yep!

Deli (*gives him a twenty-pound note*)   Good. Give it to the mother this evening. Tell her thanks?

Ashley   I don't need it actually, Dad.

Deli   Oh yeah?

Ashley   Yeah.

Deli *snatches it back.*

Deli   Seen.

Anastasia *comes out with a tray of food. While speaking, she fills up the cabinet.*

Deli   Anastasia, you've met my son Ashley, right?

She pauses for a second. It is as if all of a sudden her breath has become very heavy for a beat.

Anastasia   What a good-looking boy you have, Deli. No we haven't met, nice to meet you, Ashley.

Ashley (*looking her up and down*)   Wha appen?

Turns to his dad. Sotto voce.

Ashley   So what, you sex it yet?

Deli (*angered*)   Don't be stupid and have some respect.

Anastasia   Deli, I put on the pan ready to fry the plantain but I can't find any.

Deli   Oh shit!

Ashley   What?

Deli   I don't done forget to reorder the blasted plantain!

Ashley   How you gonna forget that? That's Uncle D's favourite.

Deli   I know that! Shit! Gotta run to the supermarket.

He runs to get his black jacket.

Ashley   Don't be long, you know!

Deli, *with jacket on, moves past* **Ashley**.

Deli   Ani, I'll be back in ten? Later, Digger.

Digger   Later.

As **Deli** *exits the phone rings. As* **Anastasia** *is closer* **Ashley** *indicates that she should answer it.*

Anastasia   I don't know what to say!

Ashley   You're taking an order not speeching da queen! Answer it then!

While **Anastasia** *is on the phone* **Ashley** *pours himself a brandy and begins to build up a spliff.*

Anastasia   Hello, Elmina's West Indian food shop –

Ashley   – Kitchen, takeaway and delivery!

Anastasia   Takeaway and delivery, how can I help you? No, he's out at present, you can probably catch him on his mobile, OK.

Ashley   Who was that?

Anastasia   The prison service.

Ashley (*smiles*)   Uncle Dougie's the original warrior boy. He's probably been put back in solitary.

Anastasia *suddenly remembers.*

Anastasia   Lard Jesus, the pan.

She dashes back through the swing doors.

Ashley *looks at* **Digger***'s glass.*

Ashley   You want a top-up?

Digger   Yeah. Mek it a brandy though. In fact, while you dere give me one of dem Chana ting that girl just done bring out.

Ashley *takes a Chana out of the cabinet and pours out the drink, then hands it to him.* **Digger** *already has a ten-pound note in his hand ready to pay.*

Ashley   Na, man. Dis one's on da house.

Digger   Did your father authorise you to give anyone anyting on da house?

Ashley (*pure admiration*)   No, but you ain't any old anyone.

Digger   Did your father authorise you to give anyone anyting on da house?

Ashley   No.

Digger *stares at him.*

Ashley   OK. That'll be four fifty.

He puts the money in the till but spends just a little bit too long looking at its contents. **Digger** *looks up at him. He quickly closes the till and* *gives* **Digger** *his change.* **Ashley** *then picks up the remote control for the TV.*

Ashley   You watching this?

Digger *shakes his head.* **Ashley** *changes it to VH1 music channel. There's a kicking garage video playing.* **Ashley** *starts 'chatting' with the tune. He's looking at the reflection of himself while he dances and chats.*

Ashley   Hold the mic while I flex, I'm a lyrical architect with the number-one set. Player haters get bang so what if dey get a back han' or else man will get jiggy, hear what! Man a pack him nine milli.

Digger *finishes his food and gets up to leave.*

Ashley   Digger!

Digger   Yow!

Ashley   Could I speak to you about som'um?

Digger   I'm busy.

Ashley   You don't look busy!

Digger   Looks can be deceiving.

Ashley   I know you don't like me . . .

Digger *doesn't answer.*

Ashley   But that's all good, cos you don't have to like people to do business wid dem, right?

Digger   I don't buy stolen phones.

Ashley   Very funny, but I ain't no pussy street punk.

Digger   Ah so?

Ashley   Ah so. No disrespect, this shit (*the restaurant*) is all good for my dad, but me, I wanna do big tings with my life, bredren. But mans needs a little leg-up.

Digger   Really?

Ashley *looks around to check that* **Anastasia** *is not about to enter. She is not.*

Ashley   I was kinda wondering if mans could run wid you? Give you little back-up and dat?

Digger   Wha appen' you ears dem beat up? I don't deal wid boys.

Ashley (*flash of temper*)   I ain't no fucking boy.

Digger *moves like the wind towards* **Ashley** *and punches him full in the face.* **Ashley** *hits the deck, blood flowing from his mouth.*

Digger   What did you say to me?

Beat.

Ashley (*whispers*)   I ain't no boy.

Digger   No! Did you use a Viking expletive when talking to me?

Ashley *is confused.*

Ashley (*staying on the ground*)   No . . . Yes . . . What's dat?

Digger (*cool*)   And you wanna be a bad man? Go back to school, youth, and learn. You can't just walk into dis bad man t'ing, you gotta learn the whole science of it. You step into that arena and you better be able to dance wid death til it mek you dizzy. You need to have thought about, have played wid and have learnt all of the possible terrible and torturous ways that death could arrive. And then ask yourself are you ready to do that and more to someone that you know. Have you done that, youth?

Ashley (*wiping the blood away from his mouth and finding his balls*) I stepped to you, haven't I?

Digger   Seen.

He sees **Anastasia** *enter. She stares at* **Digger** *with hate. His phone rings.*

(*Overjoyed.*) Bloodclattttttttt. Is when you reach? Haaaaaaa. Where you dere? Dem let you in the country? Bloodclattttttt.

He exits. When **Ashley** *turns and sees* **Anastasia** *he is momentarily taken aback.*

Ashley   How long have you been there?

She doesn't answer.

(*Trying to flex his manhood.*) Don't you understand English?

Ashley (*motherly*)   I just reach.

She moves towards **Ashley** *to help him up. As if to hold him. As she kneels down, he jumps up.*

Ashley   What you doing? Get off.

She steps back.

You talk anything of this and you're dead!

Anastasia   How old are you?

Ashley   Nineteen. Why? You looking for a fit young tings to wok?

Anastasia (*pointed*)   When my son was nineteen you think he would talk to a big woman like dat?

She moves away. Enter **Deli**, *with plantain box under one arm and his mobile in his hand. His face is drained of all life. He stands unable to move for a moment.*

Wha' wrong wid you?

Deli (*quietly to himself*)   They've killed Dougie. The man was practically home and they done kil . . . kill him. (*Holding his head.*) Ahhhhh.

Ashley *jumps up to comfort his father.* **Deli** *pushes him off.*

Deli (*screams*)   Oh God, dem catch me again. I could kill a bloodclaat man tonight.

Lights down.

As the lights go down we hear a haunting eight-bar refrain played on the gurkel.

Scene Three

Day. We are in the restaurant. **Anastasia** *is stacking the heated cabinets with food with one hand and reading a book.* **Ashley** *is on the phone taking an order. Seated with* **Digger** *and* **Baygee** *is* **Clifton** *(sixty-three, but looks mid-fifties). He is a large-built man with a mouth full of gold teeth. Dressed in a very flash three-piece suit, his cashmere coat is over the back of a chair. His suitcase is visible. He is a boastful man who defines himself very much by how much attention he gets from those in his immediate surroundings. There is a slight shake in his left hand from time to time. With his catchphrase 'you see',* **Clifton** *uses his eastern Caribbean accent to full effect when storytelling. He is mid-story when we join the scene.*

Ashley   It'll be with you in twenty minutes. (*To* **Clifton**.) Carry on.

He hands order to **Anastasia**. *She enters the kitchen.*

Clifton   . . . Well, you see, this man was at least six foot . . .

Ashley   Six foot . . .

Clifton   . . . five. And in dem days dere that was a giant . . .

Ashley   In any day, boy . . .

Baygee   . . . Clifton, every time you tell that story, the man has to grow two inches? . . .

Clifton   Shut up and let me tell the youth the story.

Ashley   Yeah, Baygee, let the man tell the story na.

Clifton   So, like I saying, he say to me, 'Who tell you you could speak to my woman? You want a cut arse?' Well, it so happen that them days was when the Teddy boys weren't making joke, and man had to have some defence . . .

Baygee   . . . That's right!

Clifton   . . . So I gently brush back me coat and show him my blade. One big arse heng man ting, and I said in a low Robert Mitcham drawl, 'If you is me fadder. Do it na! Let we see who is the man and who is child.' And I just leave that in the air hanging. Well, I see a flash in he eye as if he was going to rush me, *you see*, cos the eye betrays an untrained man. I go to grab me ting but something deep inside me, and I swear to this day it was the voice of my old mudder, say, 'Wait till he mek he move.' Well, let me tell you it was that voice save me old mudder having heart attack when she hear Clifton come to England to get hang. Cos he look at me but the monkey must have realised that this would have been his last night on earth cos he just let out a little 'Ha' and walk off. Not another word.

Ashley   Gwan.

Clifton   But you know what the real funny thing was about that evening? When it all done, tell me where the woman was?

Ashley   All over you!

Clifton   Gone. Nowhere to be seen. The two stewpid black men would have finish their lives over a woman that didn't give a coconut leaf about either of dem.

Baygee   Huh, dem was the days when they use to feel you bottom to see if you had a tail. Clifton, you remember what Mary Lou do you?

Clifton   Yes, but that's another story for another time.

Anastasia *with her usual look of concern in her eyes comes out with the order and places it in front of* **Ashley**. *He ignores it.*

Ashley   Raaaaaaaaa, you got stories, man, you're smooth.

Clifton   Me, na. I coarse like saltfish skin. But I believe in living life to the full, and it is only possible to live as long as life intoxicates us. As soon as we sober again, we see it all as a delusion, a stupid delusion, and death provides the only alternative.

He decks his rum in one.

Clifton   You at college, right?

Ashley *nods.*

Clifton   Who said that?

Ashley   I don't know.

Clifton   Baygee? Come on, you had the benefits of West Indian education, which European writer said that?

Baygee   Is me you asking?

Clifton (*sizing up* **Digger**)   Young fellow? Or should I say 'bad man'. You know the answer?

Digger (*cool and mellow*)   No I don't know who said that, do you?

Clifton   Now, you see, there's a clever man. Flip the script, turn the tables. The truth is I don't know either, but it sound pretty good, don't it?

Digger'*s phone goes off. He answers.*

Digger   Yow! . . .

Anastasia (*annoyed at being the only one not asked*)   Tolstoy!

Clifton (*shocked*)   What?

Anastasia   Tolstoy. The minor Russian aristocrat . . .

Clifton, *who knew all along, doesn't like being upstaged. He automatically goes into verbal slap-down mode. The speeches overlap.*

Clifton   . . . who is reputed to be Gandhi's direct inspiration. And without Gandhi, you have no Martin Luther, and without MLK you have no civil rights, and without civil rights you have no equal rights which means women, blacks, none of us would be standing on the soil we do today.

Digger   Seen . . . Seen . . . Don't fuck about, yu hear, star! Me will kill a man dead fe dat . . . Stone dead . . . Me soon come . . . Hold it right ya dere so . . . Move an inch and coffin lid have fe close.

Digger *leaves some money on the counter and begins to leave hurriedly.* **Anastasia***'s eyes follow him.*

Digger (*kisses his teeth*)   People just can't do what they suppose to do in this world, can they?

Ashley   I can!

Digger *stops and stares at* **Ashley** *for a moment. Almost instinctively, he's about to tell* **Ashley** *to come with him, but he doesn't.* **Anastasia** *stares at* **Ashley**.

Anastasia   Ashley!

He turns to her momentarily.

Ashley   What?

Digger   Mr C. Later.

Clifton *clocks this interaction.* **Ashley** *runs to the door and watches* **Digger**. *After a beat he turns to* **Clifton**.

Ashley   Sorry, carry on. I like to hear you, you're proper clever.

Clifton (*takes in* **Digger** *leaving*)   What's the point in being clever and none of you children take you foot? One end up a bloody thieve, the next a brok-hand boxer. Tell me what I did to deserve that, eh? Where me brains go, Baygee?

Baygee   Life don't go the way we want it.

Clifton (*decking his glass of rum*)   You don't lie, partner, you don't lie. Maybe you'll be the one that'll take me mind, eh, junior?

Deli *walked in near the end of the conversation with a box under his arm, but was not seen.*

Deli   Maybe he will, but that'll be because his father was around to nurture and support him.

Clifton *turns to* **Baygee** *embarrassed.*

Clifton   Oh God.

His hand begins to shake slightly. He calms it.

Hello son.

Deli *checks* **Ashley** *who is watching him closely.*

Deli   Hello, Clifton.

Clifton *and* **Baygee** *clock each other.*

Clifton   I come to pay me respects to you and help bury me first-born.

Deli   Is that so?

Clifton   I didn't mean nothin' by –

Deli   – Ashley, did you give your grandfather something to eat?

Ashley *(he's never seen his father treat anyone like this)*   Yeah.

Deli   Good. Then, Clifton, your respects are accepted and thank you for your visit.

He opens the door for **Clifton** *to leave.*

Clifton *(calm and cool)*   Oh, I haven't quite finished my food. You wouldn't put a man out on an empty belly, would you?

Deli *closes the door.*

Clifton   So I hear I'm a great-grandfather? (*Jesting.*) Bonjey! How you let the child age me so? (*Beat.*) The place don't look all dat but I hear you're doing OK? That's good!

Deli *(pointed)*   Bad luck is always just around the corner.

Clifton   Must be doing well to have bought two acres of land home!

Silence. **Clifton** *clocks that this is not public information.*

Deli   Like I said, man never knows what's around the corner.

Clifton (*changing the subject. To all*)   Eh! You know the first man I see when I reach Hackney?

Baygee   Who?

Clifton   Macknee the old Scottish man.

Baygee   Oh ho!

Clifton   I laugh till I couldn't laugh again. You see, I knew this was going to be a good trip when I saw that mean-nose bastard in a wheelchair, drunk, raggedy, throwing himself in front of people car shouting abuse.

Ashley (*shocked*)   You know the old drunken Scottish man, Grandad?

Clifton   Me use to rent a room from him. If I think hard, you fadder may have been conceived dere.

Ashley   Boyeeee, he's off his head, dread. Bare swearing and ramming people's vechs with his wheelchair. Man's due to get spark!

Anastasia   The man in a wheelchair, have some pity on him na.

Baygee   The bitch can walk. Sorry. (*To* **Anastasia**.) I mean, there's nuttin wrong with his leg.

Clifton   Is all the wickedness he do people that haunting him.

Baygee   If he was West Indian I'd say somebody wok obea him.

Clifton   Is only black people that know witchcraft?

Baygee *shrugs.*

Clifton   The most witchcraft is practise by the white man. How do the arse you think he managed to take Africa from we. That white man –

Deli *explodes 0–60.*

Deli   . . . Don't bring none of your white this and dat in here, Clifton. I don't want to hear that.

Baygee   That's no way to speak to your father, Deli.

Deli *(trying to hold it down)*   Baygee, please!

He clocks **Anastasia***'s response.*

Clifton   No, the boy's right. In his place, his word is *the* word.

Beat.

Baygee   Clifton, come let we go over to the betting shop na? The old boys in there they go shit when they see you.

Beat.

Clifton   I coming, I coming. Baygee, you mind if my son and I have a few minutes?

Baygee   Of course.

He steps to the back of the restaurant.

Clifton   I know your brother meant a lot to you. I'm sorry. But this is the way of the world.

Deli *stares at him blankly.*

Clifton   You see, death is around us everywhere.

Deli   Ah ha.

Beat.

Clifton   I need somewhere to stay just until the funeral finish.

Beat.

Clifton   I was wondering if . . . Until I see the doctor for me hand, and attend the funeral . . .

Deli *still doesn't reply.*

Clifton   I wouldn't burden you. A sofa will do. Two weeks max.

He stares right into **Deli***'s eyes.* **Deli** *thinks. He sees* **Clifton***'s hand shake. Silence.*

Deli   I can't have you stay here. This is Elmina's place. I'll call Ashley's mother and see if she'll put you up in the spare room. But once Dougie's buried I want you to leave, Clifton.

Clifton *looks at Elmina's picture and picks up his suitcase.*

Clifton   I'll be in the Black Dog across the road. When you ready, send for me. (*Taking in* **Deli***.*) Baygee, come na! The boys go say, 'Big time Clifton, what you doing back in England, boy?' And I go tell them the Queen send for me. You mind if I leave my suitcase here?

Baygee   How you could ask the child that? Of course he don't. Come, boy.

Clifton   I coming. I coming.

Baygee   Stop coming and come.

They leave. **Ashley** *takes the food to deliver off the counter and looks at his father before leaving. As if paralysed,* **Deli** *stands rooted on the spot.* **Deli** *looks up to the picture of his mother. He is disappointed in himself for not outrightly refusing* **Clifton***.*

Deli (*whispers to Elmina*)   I tried.

Anastasia   Your pops is a character eee!

Deli   Before I knew myself, I knew I was Clifton's child.

Anastasia   They fuck you up, your mum and dad.

Deli   That's what Digger says about women.

Anastasia   You think that too?

He shrugs.

(*Innocently.*) Do you get on with Ashley's mother?

Deli   I'd rather not talk about her actually.

Anastasia   OK.

Silence.

How did the meeting go?

Deli   'To find the information needed to start the case would be' – how did they put it? – 'cost prohibitive' was the common phrase. Everybody knows your last day in prison you keep you fucking head down. But Dougie, no! He was a troublemaker, Anastasia, that's why no one wants to take the case, no one that I could afford right now anyway.

Anastasia   He left you money, right?

Deli   Sorry?

Anastasia   Dougie left you a whole heap ah money, right, everybody knows dat.

Deli *doesn't answer.*

Anastasia   Even if you have to spend you last cent, find someone. You can't mek people kill you family and left it so! There must be somewhere else you could go?

Deli *flashes a steely glance.*

Deli (*flash of anger*)   No, there is not somewhere else I can go, I have been everywhere, alright?

Beat.

Anastasia   You know that tone you just employed, you're sure that's the choice you wanna stick with?

Deli   Pardon?

Anastasia   Cos I don't know what kind of women you are use' to but, baby, I don't let men speak to me like that?

Awkward silence.

Deli   Sorry.

Anastasia   Apology accepted.

Beat.

Anastasia *runs over to her bag and gets out her* Acts of Faith. *She rips out a page.*

Deli   What you doing?

She sticks it to the counter.

 You don't find there's enough posters on the wall? What's that, Anastasia?

Anastasia   It's a page I don't need any more.

She enters into the kitchen through the swing doors, whistling. **Deli***, intrigued, gets up and reads the page. Shaking his head, he laughs while reading it.*

Deli (*kissing his teeth*)   What rubbish . . . rubbish.

Anastasia *pops her head over the swing doors. The dialogue tumbles over each other.*

Anastasia (*surprised*)   Why's it rubbish?

Deli *walks away.*

Deli (*taking the piss*)   'In every disaster lies a lesson' . . .

Anastasia   It's true . . .

Deli   . . . 'If you can truly learn that lesson' . . .

Anastasia (*increasingly frustrated*)   . . . I know it in my own life . . .

Deli   . . . blah blah blah . . .

Anastasia (*vexed now*)   . . . It ain't no blah blah blah, this is, this is, life-healing stuff . . .

Deli   . . . Healing? What you healing for? . . .

Anastasia (*firm and straight*)   . . . So when the good tings come along you're ready?

Deli (*vexed*)   Good tings don't happen to me, Anastasia . . .

Anastasia   What stupidness . . .

Deli   . . . Ah my life me ah talk 'bout you na! And you know what me discover? Man is not suppose to want. I wanted, I could have been da don, and what happen? Bam, it get mash. I wanted to, I fucking worked hard to be there with Ashley and his mum! Bam, it get mash. I wanted my brother home, here with me and what happen? One step from the fucking gate, bam, he get mash. Don't tell me about my life.

Anastasia (*bitter*)   Oh you's one feeling sorrow for yourself, motherfucker?

Deli   What? . . .

Anastasia   You have things others dream of. This place . . .

Deli   . . . This place! Tell me what's so great about this place? I have a handful of customers who spend five pound a shot and talk nonsense all day! What did you say I have again?

Anastasia   You have you child. 'Anyting better than having you child –' How could anyting good happen to you when you don't look after the shit you have.

Beat.

Deli (*angry*)   And how am I suppose to do that?

Anastasia (*growls with passion, close up to his face*) You supposed to clean up your environment, Deli. This restaurant stinks. People walk in here, they smell Digger and walk straight back out. I've seen it. But you, my friend, you're comfortable with the stench of death around you?

Deli   There's nothing wrong with Digger that a couple of years' intense hard labour wouldn't put right.

Anastasia   If you're gonna joke forget it. You mek me tired.

Deli   You know that tone you just used with me? Do you always talk to your bosses like that? Cos I ain't use to my employees taking to me like that!

Anastasia   You know what? You're right.

Anastasia *walks to get her coat.*

Deli   Where you going?

Anastasia (*screams visibly upset*)   Why are my men too weak to raise their head above the fucking water. I don't want to be around another loser, Deli! I lose too much in my life already.

She's putting on her coat.

Deli   It's cos Digger's in here that them other punks don't come looking for money.

Anastasia (*stops*)   What money?

Deli   Ah, so there's something's you don't know, Oprah? Protection money.

Anastasia   You pay protection money?

Deli   No, that's the point. So Digger helps me, OK!

Anastasia (*tired*)   Whatever, Deli, whatever!

Coat in hand she makes to leave. **Deli** *thinks for a moment.*

Deli   Hold up na!

She carries on walking.

Deli   Do you like plantain?

Anastasia (*stops unsure where he is heading*)   Ummm! Sure!

Deli   Well, wait na!

He enters the kitchen leaving her outside now. He laughs.

Huh! Look up there, what do you see?

Anastasia   Ummmmm, picture of your mother?

Deli   That was the last person to talk to me like that and still have dem head.

Beat.

'We have entered a stranger's dream, and for trespassing he has rewarded us with his worse nightmare' is what my father use to say about living in England.

Anastasia   He come back here though, innit?

Deli *enters with two 'plantain burgers' and hands one to* **Anastasia**.

Deli   Da da! You ever had a plantain burger before?

Anastasia   No!

Deli   Here, try this. Breast of chicken, sitting on crisp lettuce with three slices of succulent plantain, all in a sesame toasted bun.

Anastasia   I hope you're not trying to obea me!

They laugh. She takes a bite.

Anastasia   Ummmmmmmmmmm!

Deli   Good, huh?

Anastasia   Yeah, almost as good as my macaroni pie!

Beat.

Deli   About a week before Clifton left, right, I was about ten and it was around midnight, I had the munchies bad. So I went downstairs and looked in the pot. There was one piece of juicy-looking chicken. But I didn't fancy that by itself so I opened the fridge door and there it was, a plantain. So I took it out and commenced to fry. (*Laughing at the remembrance.*) And it came out alright. I jammed that chicken in a bun and threw the burnt-up plantain on top ah it and boyyyyy that ting taste gooooood. I was so digging on that bun, I had forgotten to switch off the frying pan. And yeah, it went up. Blacked up the whole kitchen. Mum and Dad heard me scream and ran down. Eventually, Dad put out the pan. My mum was just pleased that I had survived but first thing my dad did when the smoke had cleared was open the chicken pot. When he saw it had gone he ran upstairs and got his belt boy and beat my claat. He said it was because I nearly burnt down the kitchen, but I know it was because of the chicken breast.

Anastasia *laughs.*

Deli   I haven't made it since then.

Anastasia (*excited*)   Deli, you's a fool. You know you have the answer right here, you know?

Deli   What?

Anastasia (*excited*)   Blouse and skirts, West Indian fast food! That's wicked. You sell dis and do up a place likkle bit and different mans would come into your restaurant. I take back all I said, damn, I knew I liked you for a reason.

She throws her arms around him. He's unsure how to react.

Deli   You can't take back! . . .

Anastasia   . . . Yes I can! . . .

Deli   . . . No you can't . . .

Anastasia (*close to his face*)   . . . Yes I can . . .

She kisses him. He kisses her back. After a few beats, though, he violently stops and pulls away.

Deli   Na, na. Sorry.

Anastasia (*searching for his eyes, trying to convince*)   It's OK . . .
I liked it.

He walks to the other side of the counter. **Anastasia** *steps back, a
little rejected.*

Anastasia   What's wrong?

Deli *doesn't respond.* **Anastasia** *walks to him, gently puts her
hand on his face again.*

Anastasia (*without emotion*)   I'll do the wanting.

Deli (*vexed, moves away*)   No, I can't do this. You're not a
bore-through gal, Ani.

Anastasia   Well then, don't just bore through.

Deli   I ain't got nothing else to offer you right now.

She doesn't reply.

(*Angry.*) The boys are betting on when I'm gonna fuck you,
Anastasia! Ashley's betting.

Anastasia   I don't watch what other people think.

She slowly pulls **Deli***'s head to face her and kisses him gently on the
mouth. He kisses her back. Just as the shop bell rings he pulls back,
holds her face in his hands and stares at her carefully.*

Enter **Digger***. He looks well vexed. Frustrated,* **Anastasia** *walks
and stands near the swing doors to the kitchen.* **Deli** *is unsure what*
Digger *has seen.*

Deli (*embarrassed, says the first thing that comes into his head*)
Hey! You're back?

Digger (*snaps back*)   What kind of question is that? Of
course I'm back. Give me a cocoa tea.

Anastasia *exits to the kitchen, shaking her head. Silence.*

Digger (*convincing himself*)   Me have fe talk it. Me just have
fe talk it. I'm not vex, you nah, I'm vex na pussyclaat. I just
had to deal with tricky. The fool na just switch pon me!

Deli *is not really that interested. He looks in the direction of the kitchen.*

Deli   Switch?

Digger   Switch, that's what I fucking said, innit? Switch! He na go collect money that is mine, and give it to Renton crew as a 'gift-offering'.

Deli   Wha?

Digger   Yes, gift, so that they would accept him inna dem crew! My fucking money! What the fuck is happening around here? I had to mark him str –

Deli (*holding his hand in the air to stop* **Digger**)   – Yo! Digger –

Digger   – Don't cut me in mid-flow! You na hear what the advert say – it's good to talk. Me, I need to get this off my chest. Anyway, when me finally hunt down Tricky I tek out my blade – the long one with the bend on the top – and me slice –

Deli   – Digger, don't pollute up my vibes wid dem talk dey – !

Digger (*exclaims*)   . . . Pollute?! Deli, you went to prison for GBH, on three men and their dogs. How de fuck I gonna pollute you?

Deli (*losing it a little*)   A restaurant is not the place to discuss fucking murder.

Digger   Where else me suppose to talk about it? On the street?

Deli   Digs, right now I don't care, just not in here, not today.

Digger   I didn't murder him, I just cu –

Deli (*shouts*)   Digger! You can't hear me? I said I don't want to hear about it. If you can't hear me, man, come out!

Digger (*disbelief switches to cold*)   What? Of your restaurant?

Deli (*a little defensively*)   I ain't saying that, Digger, I'm just saying, what if someone walked into the place and overheard this kind of talk? They'd have heard all your bizness. You didn't even check, you just come in and start fe talk. Suppose 5.0 was in here?

Digger   But they ain't! Nobody comes inside here.

Deli (*losing it a bit*)   Well maybe that's the problem. Look, I don't want no dirty talk inside yere, take from that what you want.

Beat.

Digger   Well, I shocked, Deli. When you does call me ignorant I don't like it but I take it, but now my talk is not good enough for you and your restaurant? Me that sit down in here for a lifetime, is not good enough? . . . .

Deli (*tired*)   . . . I didn't say that, Digger.

Digger   Seen, so you, like all them other niggers round here, switching on me?

Anastasia *comes to the swing door.* **Deli** *looks to her.* **Digger** *looks to her.*

Deli   Let me get some more cocoa from the back.

Deli *and* **Anastasia** *clock each other for a moment before exiting into the back, leaving* **Digger** *in the restaurant alone.*

Digger (*vexed, to himself*)   Keep your fucking tea. Ah wha de?!

Ashley *enters.*

Ashley   Yes! Digger!

Digger *turns to* **Ashley**. *He pauses for a moment. Looks to see if* **Deli***'s about. He's not.*

Digger (*slow but over-friendly*)   Yes, Ashley, what gwan?

The lights slowly fade.

Act Two

The lights are down. We hear the voices of all the characters sing a slow blues called 'You Gotta Move'. While they are singing the lights slowly rise so that we can just about make out the figures. Facing upstage, the characters are at Dougie's funeral. Set to the side is a lone female figure in traditional African headgear playing the gurkel.

All
> You may be rich
> You may be poor
> You may be young
> You may be old
> But when the Lord gets ready you ga'da move
>
> You may be black
> You may be white
> You may be wrong
> You may be right
> But when the Lord gets ready you ga'da move
>
> You ga'da move
> You ga'da move
> You ga'da move child
> You ga'da move
> And when the Lord gets ready you go'da move
> And when the Lord gets ready you go'da move

The lights fade during the final chorus.

Scene One

Restaurant. Night, three weeks later.

Lights snap up on a refurbished restaurant. It looks good. The newly painted walls no longer have any posters. And the stools have been replaced by new Ikea-type modern ones. The only thing that remains is the picture of Elmina above the swing doors. And the TV, which is on. Above Elmina's picture, however, is a new sign that reads,

'ELMINA'S PLANTAIN HUT'. On the back wall is a picture of Dougie with the words 'Dougie Andrews, 1959–2003 RIP. They have just had the opening-night party. **Deli** *is closing the door behind the last customer / party attendee.* **Anastasia** *is clearing away the glasses and plates of food.* **Baygee** *and* **Clifton***, who are well tipsy, are sitting at the counter.* **Baygee** *is playing his guitar and* **Clifton** *is singing loudly to the calypso rhythm being played. As he sings his eyes follow* **Anastasia***.* **Deli** *is in buoyant mood.*

Clifton (*sings*)
 Jooking, Jooking, Jooking
 Gal her you bottom do so much stunt
 Jooking, Jooking, Jooking
 Let we try disting from de front
 Jooking, Jooking, Jooking
 I hope it's good seed you does lay
 Jooking jooking till de break of day.

Deli   Clifton, stop dat na, man.

He shouts to the customers that have just left. He is in new businessman mode.

Deli   Bye, thanks for coming. Don't forget for each ten burgers ordered you get the eleventh free . . . OK . . . Thanks again.

Clifton *mocks him to* **Baygee**.

Clifton (*sings*)   For each ten burgers ordered you get the eleventh free! (*Speaks.*) Black people buying ten ah anyting, eh, Baygee?

Ashley (*swigging from champagne bottle, he looks at his watch nervously*)   Right, that's the family ting done!

Deli (*friendly*)   So what, you can't help me clean up the place?

Ashley   What?!

Anastasia   Thank you for helping, Ashley, tonight, Ashley.

Ashley *doesn't quite know how to react, so quickly smiles.*

Deli *turns to* **Clifton**.

Deli   And I hope you're proud of yourself?

Clifton   What happen to you?

Deli   The need for you to get on the table, start singing blasted rude calypsos and running the blasted customers was what. It was supposed to be an upmarket launch.

Beside herself, **Anastasia** *laughs under her breath.*

Clifton (*taking the piss*)   Upmarket launch? It was a party! And when man have party people suppose to dance, not stand up and chat. What de arse this generation coming to?

Deli   It's the opening of a new West Indian restaurant, Clifton, not a blasted Shebeen!

Clifton   There was nothing West Indian about it. You have a master calypsonian sitting right here, you know, and would you let him play? NO! We had to mek coup in the name of culture and take matters into we own hand.

Deli (*matter-of-fact*)   No disrespect, Baygee, but that was not the image we (*looking at* **Anastasia**), I, want people to connect with this restaurant. It's a new vibes we ah deal in right now.

Anastasia   Listen, the man from the council pre-ordered a month's delivery of plantain burgers for black history month and paid upfront. We should be proud ah we ourselves. West Indian fast food reach.

Just as she is about to hug him, he steps back, takes the bottle of champagne away from **Ashley** *and returns to* **Anastasia** *with a glass.*

Clifton   If you ask me, fast and West Indian is a contradiction in terms.

Deli (*to* **Anastasia**)   Here.

Anastasia (*pointed*)   I've had too much already. Any more and you'll have to carry me home on your back.

Deli   Drink the drink na. Tonight is well special, it's also my bir . . .

Baygee *changes to an old-time kinky reggae rhythm.* **Clifton** *instantly recognises it, stands on the stool and starts to sing at the top of his voice.*

Clifton (*sings*)
  Soldering ah wha de young gal want, soldering.
  Welding ah what de young gal want, welding.

Deli   Jesus!

Ashley (*nervously checks his mobile*)   Gwan, Grandad.

Deli   Clifton, will you stop you noise?

He stops momentarily.

Clifton   What de arse do this, boy?

Kisses his teeth.

Anastasia   Maybe you should call your dad and Baygee a taxi!

Clifton *is offended by* **Anastasia***'s comment.*

Clifton   What you trying to say, I is drunk?

Deli   Finish up you drinks, Clifton, home time.

Clifton   Answer me this! Can a drunk man extemporise?

Anastasia   I don't know, Clifton?

Clifton (*concentrating hard*)   Well, think about it. See! You can't answer because, the answer would be contri, contradictory to your current thesis.

Anastasia *laughs.*

Clifton   Baygee! Prepare me a rhythm.

Deli   Oh man!

Baygee *starts to play an old-time calypso rhythm.*

Clifton   You ready? You ready? Young boy, give me a subject quick while the rhythm hot! Quick!

Anastasia *pours herself a drink.*

Ashley   Um, um football! Football!

Clifton   Here we go. They use to call me culture master. Be prepared to get teach. (*Sings.*)
    History is a funny thing,
    History is a funny thing,
    Listen to me, people,
    Cos is about football me ah sing.
    Clive Best the greatest,
    Baller West Ham ever had,
    But from the stands they'd shout each game,
    Go home you black bastard.

Deli   Oh here we go!

Clifton (*sings*)
    Oh England, what a wonderful land,
    In England what you must understand,
    Is whatever you do, wherever you rise,
    Please realise, you could never disguise.
    You's a black man in a cold cold land.

Deli   That isn't about football! It's you on your high horse again.

Clifton (*vexed*)   Did you hear the word football?

Deli   Yeah . . .

Clifton (*turning to* **Ashley**)   . . . Did you hear the name of a footballer?

Ashley   Yes.

Clifton   Den it was about football, wasn't it?!

Ashley   Grandad, you give me jokes, boy!

Deli   I'm going to put the rubbish outside and I'm calling you a taxi, Clifton.

Anastasia   I'll help you!

Deli (*softly*)   You ain't paid for dem kinda work dere, girl.

Anastasia *exhales quietly.*

Clifton   Sweet gal, give me a subject na!

Anastasia   Um, love.

Clifton   That easy, man. Something hard.

Anastasia   OK. Trust!

Clifton   Alright, you ready now? Slow down the rhythm, Baygee.

Baygee   Oh God, man, you's a dictator!

He slows down the rhythm. **Clifton** *sings.*

Clifton
I look at you, you have eyes that I could trust,
The way you look me up and down on da number seven
bus . . .

Baygee (*disgusted*)   Number seven bus?

Clifton (*quickly*)   Shut up. (*Continues to sing.*)
I think you is a lady,
But I don't know maybe,
Tonight if you'll give yourself to me.

(*Chorus:*)
Give it to me

Baygee (*sings back-up*)
Give it to me.

Clifton   Give it to me.

Baygee   Give it to me.

Clifton   Nice and soft, soft and hard, give it to me.

Baygee   Give it to me.

Clifton   Give it to me.

Baygee   Give it to me.

Clifton   Cos tonight you'll live you fantasies.

He ends kissing **Anastasia***'s hand.* **Ashley** *applauds.*

Anastasia   Clifton, that was rubbish, but you're brilliant!

Clifton *turns to* **Baygee***.*

Clifton   Don't stop, boy, eh, eh, you losing you touch!

He grabs **Anastasia** *by the hand to dance with him.*

Anastasia   No, no!

Clifton   Get up, girl.

She gets up.

Baygee, sing one of them love song you use to play when we
was young na!

Baygee *starts to sing.*

Baygee   Darling, I can feel you sweet aroma, etc. etc.

While **Baygee** *is singing* **Anastasia** *makes to leave, but* **Clifton**
pulls her close to him. They slow-rub.

Anastasia   You're very strong for a, a, a older man.

Clifton *smiles.*

Clifton   Iccceeettch! It's been a long time.

Anastasia   Since you danced with a woman?

Clifton   Since *you* danced with a man. I can tell a
woman's history by simply touching her. See, when I *grabbed*
you, you flexed vex but now that I hold you softly, you don't
know what to do with yourself, do you?

Anastasia   You are very sure of yourself!

Clifton   Am I wrong? Or am I wrong?

Beat.

Anastasia (*matter-of-fact*)   Actually, you're not. I haven't had . . . let a man touch me with tenderness for a lifetime.

Clifton   Why?

Anastasia   Cos men kill things.

Clifton (*ignoring*)   What about my son, hasn't he touched you with, how you say, tenderness?

Anastasia   I don't think your son is interested in me that way. I'm a bit old for him, Clifton.

She loses her balance. **Clifton** *holds her.*

Oh!

Clifton   Where as I, on the other hand, *like* a sprightly young thing?

Anastasia *stands and then steps away from him.*

Enter **Digger**. *He pops his head round the door. As soon as* **Ashley** *sees him he drops the champagne glass he has in his hand. Everyone clocks this, except* **Clifton** *who is still deadly focused on* **Anastasia**.

Digger   So all you have big-time party and nobody doe invite me?

Clifton   Eh, eh, Digger, where you been, I thought you was dead!

Digger (*cold*)   Wha! You miss me?

Ashley *moves out.*

Ashley   Laters, people.

He touches **Digger** *with his fist very casually.* **Digger** *nods back again very casually.* **Ashley** *gone.*

Anastasia   Ashley, where you go (ing? . . .)

Enter **Deli** *from the back.*

Deli   Ashley!

He sees **Digger**. *He is slightly taken aback.*

Deli   Yo! Digger. Good to see you, man. What gwan?

Digger (*very cool*)   Just cool, yu nah! Hmmmm, all you fix up the place good.

Deli   Thanks. Want a burger or something?

Digger   Nah. Dem fast ting dere just give a man wind. Innit, Clifton? . . .

Clifton   . . . You doe lie, you doe lie.

Deli   I could probably cut up some chicken, stew it up and put it in a bun or something?

Digger   Nah, man, I wouldn't want you to mess up you new kitchen and dat. Anyway, just passing, yuh na! Later.

Clifton   Digger, where you going!? You don't hear me sing yet?

Digger   When business calls, Clifton!

Digger's *gone.*

Deli   Where's Ashley?

Anastasia   He just popped out.

Deli (*contained anger*)   Jesus.

Deli *picks up his mobile and speed-dials.*

Anastasia   Deli come and dance man, deal wid de rubbish later.

It's engaged. **Deli** *kisses his teeth.*

Deli (*still elsewhere, cold*)   . . . I don't have time for that! I don't Clifton, your taxi's gonna be about five minutes. Gonna have to share one with Baygee, they're running low!

He exits.

Anastasia   Clifton, something look wrong wid me? Excuse.

She leaves for the toilet. **Clifton** *sits next to* **Baygee**. **Baygee** *is looking at the swing doors, thinking of* **Deli**.

Clifton   You see she, dirty gal that!

Baygee   What you talking about, man?

Clifton   You don't see how she push up she hot tings pon me!

Baygee (*with a drunk man directness, still strumming*)   You too nasty! I know you, you know! Take you eyes off the man woman.

Clifton (*all innocence*)   Is not the boy woman yet. Anyway, there's only two woman in the world I wouldn't trouble, me modder and me sister. And both ah dem dead.

Baygee *cuts his eyes at him.*

Baygee   I find since you come back that boy turn cold, you know.

Clifton (*kissing his teeth*)   Man should be glad not mad to see him fadder. In my day . . .

His hand is shaking.

Baygee   . . . Eighteen years is a whole heap ah time . . .

Clifton   . . . Too fucking soft. What happen between his mother and me is between his mother and me. He's a fucking divorced man, he should know that.

Baygee (*goes into performance*)   That's why I never marry, you know. I like a cat, I hunt alone, eat alone and the only time I want to be stroked is when I giving 'thunder'.

Clifton   Alas, a good philosophy, but too late for me.

Baygee   What is really wrong wid you, Clifton?

Clifton   Ah, a little sugar, little pain in me foot dem. Nothing I can't lick.

Baygee   Yeah?

Clifton   Personally, I blame the white man.

Baygee   Oh gosh, how you reach there, boy?

Clifton   Is true. People who feel discriminated against, you see, have higher blood pressure, die earlier, have more heart disease and die of cancer in higher numbers. Dem prove it. There's a test case in America right now that women bringing against men.

Baygee (*not really interested*)   So you sick bad?

Clifton   Baygee, a batman's can be called out several ways. Caught in the slips, clean bowl like a fool swinging for a huge six . . .

Baygee   . . . That's the way I want to go . . .

Clifton   . . . or he can get LBW'd. But it's not until the umpire raise he finger so, that you leave the crease. An he don't even look in my direction yet. Heaven go have to wait, boy.

He raises his glass. The men finish off their drinks. **Baygee** *plays the guitar. We hear the toilet flush.*

Baygee (*sings*)   Here's to life, joy and prosperity, may I be in mid-stroke when death call on me.

(*Speaks.*) Wooooooooooow! How that ting does just spring up on you so. The other day man was in full action when all of ah sudden me feel like me have to piss.

Clifton   You should'a let it out! She wouldn't ah know.

Baygee   Shut up, man. You too damn nasty.

Baygee *runs to the toilet.* **Anastasia** *enters. She has a rejuvenated sensual air about her.* **Clifton** *puts his head in his hands and lets out a slight groan. She stops when she hears this.*

Anastasia   I know that sound.

Clifton *looks up, surprised.*

Clifton   You do?

Anastasia   You don't fool me, Clifton. I can hear the pain.

Clifton   . . . Pain? . . .

Anastasia   . . . Of losing your first-born . . .

Clifton   It's the cramp in me foot actually. The diabetes does bring it on terrible.

Anastasia   Oh!

Clifton   But I'm glad you're concerned. Listen, I'm a direct man. You look good and I look great. What you say we keep each other company tonight? It's a long time since I really talk to a woman, maybe you show me how to grieve?

She understands loud and clear what he is trying to say.

We hear the loud tooting of the minicab.

Baygee *enters the room doing up his flies.*

Baygee   Ah, lovely! The only thing that can compare to sex! A good leggo water.

Enter **Deli**, *with a very dirty heavy carrier bag. He puts it under the counter.*

Deli   That will be your cab, gentlemen. Ani, you have to jump in with the guys, they're out of cabs.

Anastasia   It's OK! Do you want me to wait till you finish what you doing and you can drop me?

Deli   No, I can't do that. Get in the cab.

Anastasia *stares at him hard.*

Anastasia   Fine, I will. Clifton, you ready?

Clifton *jumps up.*

Clifton   Right, let's not keep the driver waiting. Your carriage awaits you, madam.

She quickly puts on her coat. She doesn't look at **Deli**. *She exits.*
Baygee *has finished packing away his guitar and has his coat on.*

Baygee   Deli, sometimes when tings staring you in the face you must take it you know. I gone!

Clifton *and* **Baygee** *exit.*

Deli *spots* **Anastasia**'s Acts of Faith *book. He runs to the door. We hear the car door slam and the cab drive off.* **Deli** *walks back in. Book in hand, he switches off the TV, gets the keys out of his pocket and is about to lock the door when* **Ashley** *barges in.*

Deli   What the arse!

Ashley   Sorry, Dad, I didn't see you there.

Ashley *is making his way through to the kitchen. He is slightly hyped.* **Deli** *searches for something to speak to him about. Before* **Ashley** *disappears behind the swing doors it comes.*

Deli   Hey, Ash, what date is it today?

Ashley   Oh shit, it's your birthday!

Deli   Yeah.

Ashley   Oh shit, sorry, Dad.

Deli   It's all good. The event tonight was my party. That's why I was glad that even though you've not been around much lately, you were around tonight.

Ashley   Yeah, well, um . . .

Deli   Come, let we break some bread together na, just you and me!

Ashley   Well, I kinda wanted to go up . . .

Deli   Stay there, I'll get us a piece of chicken each.

Ashley   Let me get it. (*Wanting to go and wash his hands.*)

Deli   Na, man, you'll only make a mess.

Ashley (*shrugging shoulders*)   Alright.

Ashley *sits by the counter. He picks up some napkins and wipes his bloody hands.* **Deli** *exits with the chicken. He puts it in the microwave.*

Deli (*entering, genuine question*)   Hey, Ashley, do you read? You know, like for fun?

Ashley   Why am I going to that?

Deli   Feed your mind maybe?

Ashley   They make all the good books into films, innit?!

Deli   Seen!

Ashley (*laughing*)   I ain't never seen you pick up a book. Oh, except *now*, yeah, you reading all bred of self-help manuals like you's a blasted white man!

Deli   Reading's for whites? I'm trying to open up my mind to different tings, what's wrong with that?

Ashley   If that's your ting, nothing, man.

The bell on the microwave indicates the chicken is heated. **Ashley** *makes to get up, but* **Deli** *moves off first.*

Deli (*exiting*)   I'll get it.

Ashley *doesn't quite get why he's being served in this way.*

Deli (*entering*)   So where was I? Oh yeah, you said there was nothing wrong with education.

He gives **Ashley** *the food.*

Ashley   Happy birthday, old man.

Deli   Thank you.

He pulls out the dirty carrier bag from beneath the counter.

Then why did I find all of your college books in the rubbish?

Deli *puts the bag next to* **Ashley**. **Ashley** *stops eating.*

Beat.

Deli *won't say another word.*

Ashley   Char! I ain't got it for this.

He gets up to leave. **Deli** *instinctively pushes him back into the chair. He backs off, but only a little.*

Deli   Why are your college books in the bin, Ashley?

Ashley   You know what? They're there, cos I put them em there!

Deli (*calm*)   Don't be rude.

Ashley (*shouts*)   I ain't got time for college!

Deli   You don't have time? What do you have time for? Fucking Machino and garage raves?

Ashley   Don't come doing this whole good caring dad number right now! . . .

Deli   . . . I've never asked you about college before now? . . .

Ashley   . . . I stand corrected, you did ask me about college, when you wanted me to take a day off to run fucking food errands . . .

Deli (*vexed*)   . . . Who you swearing at, boy . . . ?

Ashley   . . . Forget this. College does not fit into the plan I have for my life. You want to keep selling your little plantain burgers, good luck to you, may you always be happy. Me, I'm a man.

Deli *loses it. He raises his hand to hit him but pulls back at the last moment.*

Ashley   Go on na!

Deli   You'd like that, wouldn't you? Yes, you'd like me to punch your lights out, so you could walk street and say, 'See, see, I told you man dad weren't no punk.'

Ashley   Why would I say that? You are a punk.

Deli   Don't you push me!

Ashley   And what? . . .

Deli   . . . And *what*? . . .

Ashley   . . . Yeah, what you gonna do, with your old self?

Deli   . . . Take you the hell out . . . (*He pulls back.*)

Ashley (*laughs*)   . . . You're joking bredren. You can't touch me! . . . I'll deck you before you can raise your hand star.

Beat.

Deli (*trying to defuse*)   And how you gonna put your hand on your father and think that you gonna live good?

Ashley   Man lives how he can.

Deli   Ah so?

*Suddenly he springs forward and grabs **Ashley**'s arm before he can move. He twists it behind **Ashley**'s back.*

Do it then! If your name is man, put your hand on me! . . .

Ashley   . . . Ahhhhhhh . . .

Deli   . . . No, not ahhhhh, put your hand on me!

Ashley   . . . Get off . . .

Deli (*firm*)   You know what I read in one of those 'white' books the other day? The true sign of intelligence is how man deals with the problems of his environment . . . (*Shouts.*) . . . I don't want to live like this, Ashley, it ain't fun . . .

Ashley   . . . Get offfffffffff, you're hurting me . . . .

Deli (*from his heart*)   . . . I'm trying, I'm trying to change shit around here, but you ain't on line, bra! Where you are trying to head, it's a dead ting, a dark place, it don't go nowhere.

He releases the grip. Emotionally exhausted, he throws his hands in the air in near surrender. **Ashley** *is silent for a moment while he adjusts to the new freedom from pain.*

Ashley (*screams*)   Don't you ever touch me again! Do you hear me? Put your hand on me ever again, father or no father, you're a dead man. Do you hear me?

Deli   Calm down, Ashley. Calm . . .

He notices blood on his own hands. He scans **Ashley** *and sees that it has come from cuts on his hands. One cut is still bleeding.*

Deli   What happened to your hands?

Ashley *pulls his hands away.*

Ashley (*slightly taken aback*)   Ummmmm, cut them, innit.

Deli   Don't take the piss.

We hear the sounds of approaching sirens. **Ashley** *becomes alert.* **Deli** *notices his nervousness even though he is shielding it well. We hear them pull up.*

Are you – you're charlied to rass! (*Beat.*) What the fuck is going on Ashley?

Ashley (*losing it*)   Then don't ask me nuttin. What the hell you think this is?

Deli   I don't know, son. That is why I'm asking you?

He goes to the door and looks outside.

Bloodclaat, ah Rose's place dat ah burn so?

Surprised, he turns to **Ashley**. *After a beat* **Deli** *runs to get his coat to go out and help. We hear more fire engines pulling up.*

We'll come back to this!

Ashley (*shouts*)   You know what I don't like about you?
You don't do nothin but sit back and let the world fuck you
over. Not me, dread!

Ashley *exits.*

Deli   You coming or what?

But **Ashley** *has gone. He looks around for a beat and then rushes out.*

Lights down.

Scene Two

Restaurant. Day.

Deli *is sat by the counter, he looks a little dazed, unsettled. After a
beat or so* **Anastasia** *runs in a little flustered.*

Anastasia   Sooooo sorry I'm late . . .

Deli (*snaps back*)   No problem . . . I heard traffic was bad.

Anastasia (*ignoring him*)   . . . I overslept like a fool. It must
have been the champagne! Eh, what gwaning across the
street? When dat burn, last night?

Deli   Look so. Man, Roy's in Homerton, x amount of
burns. Rose's life work gone. That's why you got to live life
while you can, boy!

There's silence for a bit.

Deli   Hey, Ani, you're quiet today?

Anastasia   Am I? Just a little tired.

Deli *shakes his head in understanding. He wants to say something but
can't quite find the right words. Eventually it comes out.*

Deli   I cleared out Dougie's room in the flat today, you
yuh!

Anastasia   Positive move, well done.

Silence.

Deli   Ani, how old did you say your son was again?

Anastasia   Nineteen.

Deli   Look at that, huh, we must have been doing it at the same time.

*Enter **Clifton**, with an extra spring in his walk. **Anastasia** moves swiftly back into the kitchen.*

Clifton   Bonjour, good morning good morning good morning. And how is everybody this bright fine morning? Well, noontime?

Deli   Someone woke up on the right side of bed!

Clifton   Oh yes, I had a very good night's sleep.

Deli   Lucky you.

Clifton   Yes, lucky me indeed. Anybody dead across de road?

Deli   No!

Clifton   Dem is Indian, innit? Insurance man.

Deli   Clifton . . .

Clifton   . . . Anyone in the labast? I wanna bust a piss!

Deli   No.

Clifton *exits to the toilet.* **Anastasia** *enters with a new batch of burgers and fries.* **Deli** *steals a few of the chips. She starts to put the burgers and fries in their takeaway bags.*

Deli (*struggles through this*)   Ani, I was thinking, as the business expands we gonna be kinda busy. If you wanna, you could stay in the flat upstairs you know! Save you getting bus in to work every day and dat?

Anastasia *looks up at **Deli**, surprised and pleased.*

While **Deli** *is speaking,* **Clifton** *re-enters but is unseen by the other two. His face drops when* **Deli** *mentions the flat.*

Anastasia (*genuine sadness*)   Oh Deli . . .

Deli (*jumps in*)   . . . You don't have to worry, I ain't using this as an excuse to jump you bones or nothing . . .

Anastasia (*straight and fast*)   . . . Why not? I'm a woman, Deli.

Deli (*struggling*)   . . . Of course you're a woman, Ani, a beautiful one, but . . .

Anastasia   But what? You know what, I got to think this through!

Deli (*covering defeat*)   OK! . . . But the offer's there if you want it.

Anastasia (*looks lovingly at* **Deli**)   Thanks, I'll think about it!

Deli   Cool.

Clifton *makes a bold entrance.*

Clifton   Baygee don't reach yet?

Deli (*pissed*)   He won't be here for at least another hour, you want something to eat?

They clock each other momentarily.

Clifton   What! That stupidness you have there?

Deli (*not surprised*)   Alright, I got some rice and peas upstairs from Sunday.

Clifton   How all you English people does eat three-day-old food I will never know. You could never be strong like my generation.

Deli   Yeah yeah yeah.

Anastasia   I'll go and get it for you!

Deli   No, it's alright.

He exits. **Clifton** *comes and stands close to* **Anastasia**. *She moves away.*

Anastasia (*firm, fast, whispered and very violent*)   What de arse you doing? I told you not to follow me in so quickly, what the hell you think it look like?

Clifton (*not whispered*)   It look like we had something nice last night!

Anastasia   Let me tell you, what happened last night was . . .

Clifton   . . . Beautiful? . . .

Anastasia   . . . Horrendous would be closer. It was a mistake that's not going to happen again.

Clifton   Um-hum!

Anastasia   Now, can we, no, I want us to keep this between me and you.

Clifton   Um-hum.

Anastasia (*struggles*)   This, it could . . . really mash up . . . Deli and . . .

Clifton   . . . And what is it that you and my son have today that you didn't have when you whining on top of me last night?

Anastasia (*angry, looks over her shoulder*)   We never had sex!

Clifton   Damn well near as. I wonder if it could be the offer of a ready-made family that is making this conversation have an air of desperation.

Anastasia (*stutters a bit*)   What you mean by dat? I don't need no family..

Clifton   . . . Oh I think you do.

Anastasia   I have my family an believe I'm not desperate for nothin', I'd just prefer if we keep it . . . to weselves.

Clifton   And from this arrangement I get what?

Anastasia   What could I possibly give you?

Beat while he thinks.

Clifton   What you didn't last night?! But in fact you know what? I've changed my mind about that. You, young lady, have a disproportionate amount of influence over my son, and I don't like it. So I tell you what I want, I want you to leave. Leave this place before I tell Deli what you taste like, and believe, he'll put you out on your arse before I've finished.

Anastasia   I beg your pardon?

Clifton *grips her tightly.*

Clifton   My son don't need his heart broken by a dirty gal who'll lay down with any man that hold her the right way.

Anastasia (*outraged*)   Who you calling dirty gal, you bomberclaat rude.

She's about to slap him. He squeezes her arm tighter.

Clifton   . . . You think you found yourself a little sucker in Deli, eh? You stick around long enough you'll share the big money he get from he brodder? Ah ah! Too many in line for that, my friend.

Anastasia *forces herself away from* **Clifton**.

Anastasia   You're a, a, *wicked* man.

Clifton   Oh, you ain't seen nothing yet! Trust me!

We hear **Deli** *enter from the kitchen. He comes through the swing doors into the shop. He is carrying* **Clifton**'s *plate of food.*

Deli   Here. I'm not doing this again, you know. You eat what's in the restaurant from now on, or nothing at all.

Clifton *shifts the plate away.*

Clifton   If it's so you going to talk to me over a little piece of food, best you keep it.

Deli   OK! Don't eat it then.

Clifton   Gimme the food.

Anastasia   Deli, I got to run over to the Internet shop for five minutes. I really need to –

Deli   . . . It's not there any more . . . .

Deli *can see that she is upset.*

Is the council order ready?

Anastasia (*dashing out*)   Yeah, it's on the counter.

She leaves, bumping into **Ashley** *at the door. He is really dressed like a street hoodlum. She doesn't say sorry but carries on running.* **Ashley** *has a stronger stand about him, a more fixed hardness.*

Ashley   What's this world coming to, your woman bumps into me and can't even say excuse!

Deli   Don't . . . (*He catches himself.*) Listen, Ashley, about last night . . .

Ashley   Don't watch dat, I've come to get my clothes.

Deli   Why?

Ashley   How you gonna ask big man his business?

Ashley *accidentally on purpose drops his car keys on the floor. And walks on. He picks up his keys and waves them in the air singing.*

Ashley   Who am I, the gal dem love, zim zimmer, whose got the keys to a bimmer.

Deli   Whose car you thieve boy?

Ashley   I ain't thieve nothing, I bought it bra!

Deli   You bought a car?

Ashley   Yep. Cash money!

Deli (*laughing*)   What car is that?

Ashley   A bimmer . . .

Deli   A BMW!? . . .

Ashley   Yep.

Beat.

Deli   Huh! You insurance it?

Ashley   I would have, but I ran out of money!

Deli   Ohhh! So that's why you're here flashing keys!

Ashley   I ain't here asking you for nothing star. You ain't got nothing that I can't get!

Deli   You always gots to be rude innit? Drag us back!

Ashley   No old man, it's bear forward motion *I* deal in.

Deli *stares at him hard.*

Ashley   Actually you know what? You're right I was rude. Hear what! Let me tek you for ride old man, let me show you *my* world. You na mean?

Deli   Your world?

Ashley   Yeah!

Deli   You're joking aren't you?

Ashley   Sorry?

Deli   Look at you, you little monkey. Dressed up like a fucking circus clown! You want me to partake in that?

Ashley (*aside to* **Deli**)   What boy! That is poetry!

Deli   Where you get the money Ashley?

Ashley*'s phone rings. He checks the number but doesn't answer.*

Ashley   That's long talk.

Deli   Dere's nothing long about it. It's an easy question, where'd you get the money?

Ashley   Some things, when you do em right, life rewards you.

Deli   . . . life rewards you? Where the fuck (you get that shit from)?

Ashley   I'm living proof of it.

Clifton *is about to intervene but* **Deli** *stares him down at the same time and continuing with* **Ashley***.*

Deli   Do you honestly expect me to come in your car and sanction your nastiness?

Ashley (*angry*)   No, I expect you to be happy for me, happy at my progress. What I don't expect, want or need, is you fronting your jealousy with petty excuses!

Deli (*even angrier*)   Jealousy? I'm a hard-working man who's survived because I don't watch other people's tings. What makes you think I'd be envious of your stupid car, I haven't even seen it?

Ashley (*overjoyed*)   Wait till you do, it's crisp!

Deli   It can be as crisp as it wants. I want nothing to do with you and your nastiness. Come out that world, Ashley.

Beat.

Ashley (*laughs*)   You're a punk, Dad. I was giving you a chance. A chance to let the whole area know that ooooh you're Ashley's father and so we roll! But no, you want to stay small, insignificant, weak. You, you disgust me. I'll be back for my clothes.

He turns to leave. His phone rings. He answers this time with his blue-tooth headset.

Ashley (*deliberately*)   Yo! Yes, Digs . . . ? Soon come, yeah, soon come.

Deli's *face drops at the mention of* **Digger**'s *name.* **Ashley** *exits the shop.* **Clifton** *looks at* **Deli**.

Clifton   You should have at least looked at the car.

Deli *stares back at him with contempt.*

Lights down.

Scene Three

Restaurant.

The news item is playing as the lights come up.

Deli *walks into the restaurant from the kitchen. He has a huge knife in his hand. He places it under the counter. He then walks back into the kitchen and comes on with a metal baseball bat. He places that behind the front door out of sight.*

Newsreader   This is not just one isolated incident. Last month Catherine Henderson, an accident and emergency consultant at Homerton Hospital, called for staff with experience from cities such as New York and Johannesburg to join her team because NHS workers were simply not equipped to deal with the flood of gunshot wounds pouring into the department.

Deli *switches the channel back to MTV or whatever music channel he can find. As he is flicking through he passes the God channel. An American preacher is screaming out.*

Preacher   It shouldn't be no surprise our inner cities are burning up. It is the sinnnnnnns of the *fathers* bearing down on our youth.

Deli *kisses his teeth and finds the music channel. Playing is the ragga video to 'Satan Strong'. As if stiff, he moves his fists, almost warming-up style, and punches the air.*

Enter **Anastasia**. *She has a bag over her shoulder.* **Deli** *sees her and stops. He clocks the bag. He smiles.*

Deli (*surprised*)   Hey!

Anastasia   Hey!

She doesn't move from the door. Pain is etched all over her face.

Deli (*pointing to bag*)   I didn't think you were coming back. You want some help with that?

He makes to the door to pick up the bag. **Anastasia** *puts up her hand to stop him.*

Anastasia   No!

He stops.

Deli   Ani, I've been thinking that maybe I should just talk straight. What I meant this afternoon was . . .

She moves to a table and opens the bag. She begins to take out some clothes. The first thing is an Averix leather jacket.

Anastasia (*ignoring him*)   . . . This belonged to Marvin, my son. I know kids don't like wearing other people's clothes but I figured Ashley might like this . . .

Deli *is unsure why she is doing this.*

Deli   That's a wicked jacket, doesn't Marvin still . . . (wanna wear that).

Anastasia   . . . Unless you think it's bad luck to give him dead clothes?

Deli *stops in his tracks. He stares at her at first not understanding then, understanding. There's a long pause while they speak to each other without words.* **Anastasia** *finally answers the question* **Deli** *has been trying to articulate.*

Anastasia   Long.

Deli   Why . . . ?

Anastasia   I'm sorry. Tell Ashley that I hope it fits and, um . . .

Deli   You're leaving?

Anastasia *nods her reply. Their speeches overlap till they reach an emotional climax.*

Deli   Don't!

Anastasia   If you hit the canvas one more time brother, you ain't getting back up. I will hurt you Deli . . .

Deli   Is this because I asked you to move in with me? . . .

Anastasia (*flash of anger*)   No. It's because the stink around this place is getting stronger and I got to run (before it takes me down.)

Deli   But I cleaned up the place Anastasia!

The horn is honked.

Anastasia (*looking out*)   I better go. That's my cab.

Deli (*frustrated it stumbles out*)   I could, shoulda, woulda coulda right now but you know what? You got to give a brother time to turn shit around, to talk what's in his heart. You can't just walk so!

Anastasia (*tender but hard*)   Sometimes you should listen to people when they say they're no good for you. It might be the truth.

The car horn honks again. She doesn't move.

Deli (*pulling himself together*)   Right.

Anastasia   Hope Ashley likes the jacket.

She leaves. **Deli** *stands still for a moment. He doesn't quite know what to do with himself. He starts to pace up and down the restaurant fretting, frustration building. To hold back the tears he starts swing punching the air. We hear the car drive off. He doesn't notice that* **Clifton** *has entered the shop and is watching him. Eventually he falls onto one of the stools head in hands.*

Clifton   It's all right son.

Deli *springs up.*

Deli   Clifton! What you doing?

Clifton   It's all right. Do you want me to give you a little time to yourself?

Pause.

Deli   No.

Pause. **Clifton** *smiles to himself.*

Clifton   No woman no cry.

Deli   . . . I liked her . . . She could have taught me . . . things.

Clifton   Yes she could have, but listen to your father when I say she wasn't for you. She was using you for lifeboat child.

Deli (*with a little attitude*)   And how do you know that?

Clifton   I'm a man of the world . . .

Deli   Oh and I'm not? You know what? Go away! I don't need you to stand above me gloating.

Clifton   Now wait a minute, I'm trying to be sympathetic and you're insulting me? . . .

Deli   I don't want your sympathy, Clifton . . .

Clifton   . . . I'm not giving you my sympathy, Deli, I'm giving you some fatherly advise . . .

Deli   . . . Well, I don't want it! Not from the man that ran left my mother for some Irish woman.

Clifton   Oh! Well, it had to come out sometime.

Deli   Yeah, I hear that after you spend out all your money on her, she run leave you for a younger model! You think we didn't hear? We heard and we laughed.

Clifton   Well, it's good to know that the gossip express is still going strong . . .

Deli   Don't mamaguy me, Clifton. Your money ran dry. You mug me mother and now your trying to mug me.

Clifton   I didn't thieve nothing from your mother!

Deli   Yes you did. You build big house with swimming pool off my mother's savings.

Clifton   Your mother and I split the proceeds of the house . . .

Deli   . . . . that my mother put the deposit down on, that she paid the mortgage on when you spend out the money down the pub and the bookies or running next woman?

Clifton   I put down my wage packet every week on your mother's table . . .

Deli   And then thief it right back.

Clifton (*snaps*)   . . . You're a grown man, for Christ's sake, stop acting like a child and use you mind. Your mother going to tell you both sides of the story?

Deli   There is no other side to the story.

Clifton   Yes, I did leave, but why, Delroy? . . .

Deli   Irish pussy!

Clifton   I didn't have to leave my home for pussy.

Deli   Really?

Clifton (*calmly*)   If I hadn't left, Delroy, I would have died. Your mother suffocated me, child. She suffocated me . . .

Deli   . . . My mother was a brilliant woman . . .

Clifton   Yes she was. Too brilliant for me. And boy, she never let me forget it. Way I talked was too rough, way I spoke was too loud. The way I walked, the way I ate. Jesus, living with that woman was like being in an airless room. It drew all of the life from me..

Deli   . . . That's fucking rubbish, she loved you like –

Clifton   No she didn't. She was stuck with me.

This stops **Deli** *momentarily.*

Your mother was not interested in me, or any other man. You ever see her with anyone new after I left?

Deli   Raising two children on one income doesn't leave much time to fraternise with the opposite sex.

Clifton   Sex! Don't let me start, your mother hated sex . . .

Deli (*puts his fingers in his ears*)   . . . Don't wanna hear this!

Clifton   She never loved me. Not the way a wife should. And let me tell you, you and Anastasia would have walked down the same street.

Deli   Rubbish, Anastasia was the only decent thing around me.

Clifton   Decent!? That gal asked me to fuck her last night because I threatened to expose her dirty nasty ways to you. How decent was that?

Beat.

Deli (*stunned*)   What did you do?

Clifton   I fucked her to prove I was right. She was a thieving little whore who was only after you and Dougie money.

Deli   No she wasn't!

Clifton   I smelt her the moment I walked in here.

Deli *runs at his father.*

Deli   How could you do that?

Clifton   Was she your woman?

Deli   No. But you must have known?

Clifton   Which is exactly why I had to prove her to be the woman I knew she was. She was here to thieve your money. Like all of them. You don't need people like that around you, Delroy, you need people around that love you.

Deli *looks at him. Enter* **Digger**. *He's in a bad mood. He brings his Chopper bike into the restaurant.*

Digger   Boyyyyy, I just done nearly kick up this fucking ambulance man. I'm driving in my car and I hear the siren so I wait for the right spot to pull over. Instead of the man wait, he swings in front of me and then cuts across my front. The fucking man doh just clip me wing! So I jump out and instead the man say sorry, he come open up his big mouth and come call me an ignorant idiot. You know I don't like that people call me that already. I had to threaten him. You been watching too much fucking 'Casualty', mate. I'll punch down your claat. When he saw that, he calmed himself and just freed up his insurance details. Fucking chip my new TT, you know, shouldda shoot him clatt.

Clifton   Wasn't there someone in the back waiting to reach the hospital?

Digger   I don't give a bombo! Deli, give me a roti.

Deli   We don't do roti no more, Digger.

Digger   Oh yeah, me forget.

Deli *throws a glance at the baseball bat behind the door.*

Deli   Eh! The police came round about the Roy ting today.

Digger   Oh yeah? What you tell them?

Deli   What Rose told me.

Digger   Which was?

Deli   That some Yardie men in mask asking for protection money burnt down the place, after beating the hell out of Roy.

Digger   Really? She told the police that?

Deli   I told her she should. How else we gonna rid this place of such vermin.

Digger   I wouldn't have thought that would do her much good. Nobody likes an informer. Not even you.

Beat.

From what I hear she refused a reasonable deal.

Deli   Did you get my son help you in your nastiness, Digger?

Digger   What you talking about? Don't be stupid.

Deli   I don't believe you. How much odder dirty youth out there you gonna recruit, you gonna take my son? I don't want you anywhere near anything of mine again, Digger. My son, myself, my shop.

Digger   You don't? . . . You should think about that. Particularly after the recent events.

Deli   You threatening me?

Digger   No. Just reminding you of who protects who! Shit's gonna change, Deli, dey run tings now. They was going to send a next man to talk to you but I said, true say that you and me go back, that I would do it and negotiate the best price for all involved.

Deli   The best price?

Digger   Best price.

Deli   After I already pay rates, tax and employees insurance, Renton crew want me to pay protection money?

Digger   Yep. I might could a get you less but ah, pay you do.

Deli   What appen, Digger? How you gonna go and join them lowlives?

Digger   Watch you mouth, Deli.

Deli   Ha, well, run tell your new employees that no. Not me.

Digger   Don't be stupid. You don't want dem kinda friction dere.

Deli   I been here ten years, Digger, what makes you think I'm gonna start paying some 'off the boat' bloody Yard boy money that I don't have?

Digger   Because they said so. It's not like you can't afford it. Everybody knows that Dougie left you a whole heap ah money.

Deli   Dougie never left me shit. You know what? Tell them they can come burn down my place, before they get a red cent from me, that they can fuck off.

Digger   I ain't gonna tell them that, Deli.

Deli   That's your business.

Digger   No, this is. Once I say you have to pay, you pay, Deli, or else I look bad.

Deli   So it's money you want, well, here, Digger, have some money.

He empties out his pockets and throws the coins at **Digger**.

Digger   Ah wha de bloodclaat!

Clifton   Delroy . . .

Digger   Deli, calm and settle youself before I have to.

Deli   Take the money, Digger.

He throws more money that he has found by the till.

Clifton   Deli, calm the hell down.

Deli   Take the money na!

He grabs hold of the till and rips it out of the counter and throws it at **Digger**.

Take the blood money.

Digger   Deli!

Digger *goes to pull his gun out but before he can get it out* **Deli** *is at his throat with the big knife.*

Deli   Do it na! See if you could shoot me before I cut your bloody throat!

Digger   Deli, you're behaving like an arse. Calm down and move the knife from my throat unless you plan to use it this very minute.

Deli   Digger, you used my son, you used my blood, to do my neighbour. You knew the first place the police were gonna come to was here.

Digger   He wanted to defend your manhood. Is not me!

Deli   My son doesn't have to defend me, Digger.

Digger   Take the knife from my throat, Deli.

He doesn't.

Clifton   Delroy, use your mind. Take the knife from the man throat.

Digger   I told him no. But all you got on the street is your rep, bro, and my youth wants rep.

Deli   I see you close to Ashley again, Digger, and I will kill you.

He takes the knife away.

And take back your stinking BMW!

Digger *stands up.*

Digger   That's a very silly ting you jus' do. (*Beat.*) I hope you can defend that.

Digger *exits, staring* **Deli** *out.*

Clifton   Was that wise?

Deli *stares at* **Clifton** *and then backs out towards* **Digger**.

Lights down.

An intense gurkel melody plays until:

Scene Four

Restaurant. Day.

Baygee *is sat with a half-eaten plantain burger in front of him. He is mid-story to* **Clifton** *who is in the kitchen area.*

Baygee   Now you know Charlie! Twenty years he dere in this country and doe miss a day work. But that afternoon, out of the blue, he head start to hurt him bad. He beg the manager not to send him home but they order him, so he go. Well, is just by chance I meet him on the street, vex he vex. I say, Charlie boy, go home and enjoy the missus. Huh, well, is den he start to tell me ting. Apparently, before Thelma would give him anyting he had to agree to put out the bins and wash de wares and all breed ah stupidness!

Clifton   What?

Enter an aproned **Clifton** *with a tray of plantain burgers. He starts restacking the shelves.*

Baygee   Yes, blackmailing de man before she get him he tings, and even then he say, no matter what he tell her, all she doing is laying stiff so dreaming ah Trinidad. Not even a little (*he imitates a female groan of pleasure*) ahhhhh to sweet him.

Clifton   Is he that wrong, he should a grip woman long! Me I would a . . .

Baygee   Wait hear de story na! So I give him a few sweet boy tips and I send he on he way. De next time I see the man, is not in burial ground!

Clifton   You lie?

Baygee   Well, the story go that when he reach home flowers in hand and ting, he hear one set a noise from upstairs. Well, he say somebody break in and must be beating he wife. So he run into the kitchen grab one big knife and creep up de stairs so as to catch the criminal in the act . . .

Clifton   Surprise him yes . . .

Baygee   When he bust into the room, tell me what he see?

Clifton   The wife beating the man?

Baygee   Thelma head stick out the window leg cock up so, and a man half he age woking it hard from behind.

Clifton   You lie?

Baygee   I look like I lie? . . .

Clifton   What he kill de man?

Baygee   Well, he sister tell me that the wife tell she, that he just look at her, and then he look at this young stallion dat making Thelma shout ting he doe hear in he life and he heart just give up so, bang, he drop and dead.

Clifton   Just so? . . .

Baygee   Just so.

Clifton   Bonjay! Ha! Well is so he had to dead. Me old man use to say, if you have to drown you can't burn.

Baygee *downs the rum in front of him in one and salutes* **Clifton**.

Baygee   He don't lie, Clifton, he don't lie.

Enter **Deli**. *He doesn't greet either of the men. He is in a world of his own.*

Clifton   Where the France you been, boy?

Deli *looks at* **Clifton** *but doesn't reply.* **Clifton** *addresses* **Baygee** *at first.*

Clifton (*to* **Baygee**)   But look me crosses na! Delroy, you going deaf? I had to set up the shop by myself, you know. Where you been?

Deli   In a meeting.

Clifton   Meeting, what kind of meeting?

Deli   I said a meeting, OK!

Clifton   You don't know we have a business to run here. None of the things going to be ready for lunchtime, you know?

Deli   Clifton, Clifton please. We miss lunch, we miss lunch.

Baygee *looks up at the two men, checks his watch and decides it's time to leave. He takes one last shot of Clark's and slams the glass on the table and stands to go.*

Baygee (*laughs*)   Gentlemen, I promised I'd drop something before twelve o'clock.

Clifton   I go have you food ready. What time you passing back?

Baygee   No, it's OK, dey just reach back from Trinidad. She go have a little home food for me.

Clifton   Who is that?

Baygee   Ms Thelma. I gone.

He exits and leaves the shop. There's silence for a bit.

Clifton   You's still a suspect?

Deli   You see Ashley this morning?

Clifton   No! (*Beat.*) I feel rather proud, you know. We seem to be running this ting well. Don't you think?

Deli   We?

Clifton   Yes, it wouldn't be unfair to say we. In fact, you know what I was thinking? You should let me move into the flat with you, son, that way we'd always be ready!

Deli   Clifton, I'm selling this place.

Clifton   Because them Yardies want a little money from you? It's better you pay them than you run away. Men don't run, son.

Deli (*fed up of everyone questioning his manhood*)   So what do they do, Clifton?

Clifton   They stay at the crease till the umpire's hand go so. (*Pointing up and out.*) Running is never the answer.

Deli   I'm not running.

Clifton   I thought you had more brains than that, man!

Beat.

Where you going if you sell this place?

Deli   I don't know. Somewhere far.

Clifton   You going to take Ashley?

Deli   I want to.

Clifton   What about me?

Deli   What about you, Clifton?

Clifton   Aren't you going to need someone to help you run the business?

Deli   Who said anything about a business?

Clifton   What else you go do? Whose going to employ someone that has no qualifications, spent a year in jail and ran away from the one positive thing he has achieved in his life. Where's your respect?

Deli   Respect for what?

Clifton   Ashley, me.

Deli   You?

Clifton   Yes actually, me. As your father you owe me respect. The respect that says, 'Daddy I know you're not well, as your son I'll take care of you till you're strong again.'

Deli   Clifton, this is the wrong time for us to be having this debate.

Clifton (*losing it*)   No, this is exactly the right time to be having it. As a child, did I ever let you walk the street raggedy?

Deli   No, but . . .

Clifton   Exactly!

Deli   That was about you, you and your children always had to be the smartest in the street!

Clifton   Exactly, I looked after you . . .

Deli   To a point.

Clifton (*to himself*)   Once and man, twice a child. Jesus. Your generation curse. You British blacks pick up worse and leave best. Instead ah you pick up the Englishman thirst for knowledge and learning you pick up his nasty habit of dumping their old people in some stinking hole for them to rot when they are at the prime of their wisdom.

Deli   Clifton, is you that said when the doctors give you the all-clear that you going home . . .

Clifton   . . . I lied. I don't have nowhere to go, Delroy.

Deli   What do you want me to do? I can't help you, Clifton, believe me, I don't have nothing!

Clifton   You and your brother bought some land home! You got money hidden away, I know. Let's go home together na? Open a little something in town. Show them bitches that Clifton can bounce back. Clifton have something. He children amount to something. You know they does laugh at me home? Yes. Your own uncle laughs at me. 'Look,' he does say, every time he sees his daughter in the paper hug up with a next white man, 'she doing well, innit? By the way, Dougie come out of jail yet.' Laughing at my seed. Let we go home show them that my seed is something. We are somebody.

Deli   Clifton, listen to me, you are not going to want to be where I am, believe me.

Clifton (*loses it*)   Don't say that!

He begins to throw over the chairs and tables.

What have I got to show for my life, Delroy? Parkinson's! What do I have to do, beg you? Fight you for it?

Deli   Calm down.

Clifton   No, you fucking calm down. Calm down? Calm down? Come and make me na, think the old man can't knock you down.

He starts swinging his fists in the air. **Deli** *stares at him, bewildered. He loses steam eventually, falling to the floor.*

Ashley *enters. He stares at* **Clifton** *on the floor and the messed-up restaurant. He doesn't say a word. Eventually, he goes to help* **Clifton** *stand up.* **Clifton** *shrugs him off and picks himself up.*

Clifton   Get off me. All you generation curse. You go rot, mark my words.

He leaves the restaurant. **Ashley** *stares at his grandfather leaving.*

Beat.

Ashley   Where's he going?

Deli   I don't know.

Ashley (*cool and deadly*)   I hear you was down the police station this morning?

Deli   Yeah, how you know that?

Ashley   What did they want?

Deli   More details of your whereabouts when Rose's place was burn.

Ashley   What did you tell them?

Deli   What I have before, that you were here with me. Why?

Ashley   You sure?

Deli   Yeah!

Ashley *walks up and hugs his dad.*

Ashley   Thanks, Dad.

Deli (*slightly taken aback*)   It's alright.

Ashley   You know I was only looking out for you?

Deli *pushes him off.*

Deli   No, you were looking out for yourself. But it's my fault. Should have got you out of here years ago. But I didn't have the resource, the wherewithal . . .

Ashley   . . . What you talking about?

Deli   They know it was you. They know it was Digger. It's only a matter of time. If Roy dies they coming to get you, son, no matter what.

Ashley *is about to say something but* **Deli** *stops him.*

Deli   Ah . . . Now I know you's a big man and dat but it's up to me to protect you the best way I know how. If I was to say that I've arranged a place away from here for us, what would you say?

Ashley   I'd say why?

Deli *struggles to find the words. Eventually.*

Deli   OK. I did go to the police station today but it wasn't about you entirely.

Ashley   No?

Deli   No. I went because I've struck a deal. You . . . for Digger.

Ashley (*shocked to his core*)   Noooo! You can't have done dat? You're many things but you're not an informer, Dad.

Deli   I knew Digger was bad but, son, he's terrible.

Ashley   He does what he has to do to survive.

Deli   Don't talk shit to me. What do you want me to do, son, protect Digger and throw you to the wolves? This is about your survival, you better know.

Ashley (*sickened*)   You didn't have to inform, Dad. Where you ever going to go in the world and not have to look over your shoulder?

Deli   That's not better than being in prison?

Ashley   Is still prison, just bigger cells.

Deli   Well, I've been in a cell, son, and it is not very nice. Each generation is suppose' to top the previous one. If I have to die on the street to get you out of that dere runnings, wouldn't I be doing my job?

Ashley   I don't believe you did this?

Deli   I did, now listen to me. The police are going to arrest Digger today, but they're only gonna be able to hold him for forty-eight hours. After he's released, he's gonna know that I shopped him, then he's going to come right here and deal with me.

Ashley   You're damn right he will!

Deli   But if you speak to the police and say that you'll testify that Digger told you to do all that happened that night, we will get fifty grand and a safe house out of the country. Coupled with the money I already have, when we ready we could fly back home and live the lives of kings.

Ashley   Hackney's home.

Deli   It won't be when Digger gets out. What? He's gonna have an informer's son in his crew?

Ashley (*realisation*)   You did that on purpose?

Deli   Yes I did.

Ashley (*screams*)   I don't believe you.

Enter **Digger**.

Digger   You better do! Didn't I tell you your father would do this. Didn't I?

Deli *stands. A little afraid but ready whatever comes next.*

Digger   How did you think you were going to get away wid dis? Wha, you think you could just pull knife on me, inform pon me and me would let you get 'way?

Deli   Man has to tek his chances in life, you get me, don't you, Digger?

Digger   I get you, but what about your son? What have you done to your child, Deli? Branded him for life. Ashley, the informer's boy.

Deli *stares him out.*

Digger   What did you think was going to happen, Delroy?

Deli   Stop all the long chat, Digger, if you come to deal wid me let's get it on like men.

Digger *pulls out a packet of crack rocks and throws them on the floor. He then removes another bag from his pocket. It is pure cocaine. He opens it and, as if releasing magic dust from his hand, throws a handful at* **Deli**.

Digger   Um-um. It's not me that's gonna deal with you. You don't know what we do to informers these days, do you? Well . . .

He turns to **Ashley**.

My youth. Deal wid this properly and you go straight to the big league. Rep is everything, and yours is gonna be huge after this.

Ashley *slowly takes out his gun.* **Deli** *just stares at him.*

Ashley   You let me down, Dad.

Digger   OK, let's do the solicitor's work for him. Put one in the roof, shows we had a struggle.

Ashley *shoots the gun off in the air.*

Deli   You ready for this life, Ashley?

Digger   Alright, now point the gun at your punk-arsed dad. The one that gets beat up and does nothing, has his business near taken away and does nothing, but then informs on a brother man to the other man for what? A piddling fifty grand! I could ah give you that! Is this the type of people we need in our midst? Weak-hearted, unfocused informers? No, I don't think so. Do you, **Ashley**?

Ashley'*s hands are shaking a little. After a beat.*

Ashley   Digger, I don't think . . .

Digger (*screams at him*)   Is this the type of people we need in our midst?

Ashley   No.

Digger   OK then, raise the gun, point it.

Ashley *does.*

Digger   Good. Is your finger on the trigger?

Ashley   Yes.

Digger   Good.

Digger *pulls out his gun and shoots* **Ashley** *dead.*

Deli   Nooooooooooooooooooooooooooooooooo.

Digger *looks to* **Deli**.

Digger   Yes. Ah so dis war run!

He exits.

Deli *kneels still by his dead son. After a few beats he rises, takes the jacket that* **Anastasia** *left for* **Ashley** *and covers his body and head. With one final glance around, he stares at the picture of his mother, then walks out of the restaurant. The violent ragga tune plays as we fade to black.*